PETHIAS KATAMPI
RICH BUT
POOR

Rich but Poor

RICHES IN AFRICA, Volume 1

Pethias Katampi

Published by Pethias Katampi, 2023.

RICH BUT POOR

First edition. August 26, 2023.

ISBN: 979-8232420390

Written by Pethias Katampi.

RICH BUT POOR

Preface

My name is Pethias Katampi. I am Zambian, holder of a diploma in business administration, and soon to be a Bachelor of Business Administration graduate as I am currently in my 4th year of study. Amidst the challenges of academic pursuits and the aspirations for a brighter future, I found myself deeply moved by the current situation in Africa – a continent brimming with potential yet grappling with the paradox of being "Rich but Poor."

As I contemplated the stark contrasts that define Africa's reality – the abundance of natural resources juxtaposed with persistent poverty – I felt an innate calling to understand the complexities that have shaped this reality. The spark to write the book "Rich but Poor" was ignited, driven by a fervent desire to shed light on the underlying factors that have hindered Africa's progress and to envision a path towards a prosperous future.

In the journey of crafting this book, I delved into the annals of history, sought insights from experts, explored diverse perspectives, and listened to the stories of ordinary Africans. Each revelation and experience only reinforced the urgency and importance of the task at hand.

As an aspiring business administrator, I realized that the issues facing Africa transcend the economic realm and are deeply intertwined with political, social, cultural, and historical dimensions. The resource curse, governance challenges, the impact of foreign involvement, and the role of religion and culture all intersect in shaping Africa's present reality.

Drawing inspiration from the stories of resilience and determination that characterize Africa's people, I embarked on a journey of introspection and exploration. Through this process, I discovered that the power to transform Africa lies not just with leaders and policymakers but also within the collective will of its citizens.

In the chapters that follow, I endeavour to present a comprehensive and empathetic analysis of the challenges that confront Africa. From the depths of historical injustices to the complexities of contemporary governance, "Rich but Poor" seeks to confront uncomfortable truths while holding on to the unwavering belief that positive change is attainable.

As I write these words, I find solace in the fact that my journey towards higher education mirrors Africa's own pursuit of progress. Just as I strive to earn my Bachelor of Business Administration, Africa too seeks to unlock its full potential and secure a prosperous future for its people.

In these pages, I invite you to join me on this transformative journey. It is a journey that calls for solidarity, compassion, and shared responsibility. As we explore the complexities of Africa's wealth and poverty paradox, we must remember that this is not just a story of a continent in crisis but also a testament to the strength, ingenuity, and resilience of its people.

I extend my heartfelt gratitude to all those who have supported and inspired me along this path – my family, friends, mentors, and fellow students. Your encouragement has been a guiding light as I venture into the world of writing and academia.

May "Rich but Poor" serve as both an invitation and a catalyst for dialogue, action, and change. Together, let us envision a future where Africa's abundance is not just confined to its natural resources but flourishes in the prosperity and well-being of its people.

With hope and determination,

Pethias Katampi

July 30th, 2023

RICH BUT POOR

5

Pethias Katampi

Table of Contents

1. **Introduction**
    - Setting the stage: Africa's wealth of natural resources, the paradox of abundance, and deprivation.
2. **African Natural Resources and Sustainable Development**
    - Overview of Africa's natural resources.
    - Challenges in sustainable resource management.
    - Principle 1: Responsible Resource Management for Equitable Development.
3. **Religion, Social Harmony, and Inclusive Growth**
    - Historical and cultural role of religion in Africa.
    - Religious practices and their effects on society.
    - Principle 2: Promoting Tolerance and Interfaith Dialogue for Social Cohesion.
4. **Governance, Corruption, and Effective Resource Allocation**
    - Unveiling the Grasp of corruption.
    - Greedy leadership and Its Impact.
    - Principle 3: Transparent and Accountable Governance.
5. **Historical Injustices and Internal Conflicts**
    - Historical context of the transatlantic slave trade and colonization.
    - African involvement in the slave trade and consequences.
    - Analysing internal conflicts and their toll.
    - Principle 4: Fostering Unity, Cooperation, and Inclusive Societies.
6. **Empowering African Entrepreneurs and Businesses**

- Examining systemic barriers to black wealth creation.
- Success stories of African entrepreneurs.
- Principle 5: Supporting Entrepreneurship for Economic Empowerment.

7. **Reimagining Education, Skills Development, and Gender Equality**
    - Pre-colonial education and its relevance.
    - Speculating on education without colonization's impact.
    - Economic benefits of gender equality.
    - Principle 6: Equipping Citizens with Skills and Empowering Women.
8. **Overcoming Historical Economic Legacies and Healthcare**
    - Impact of colonization on Africa's wealth.
    - Examining economic policies and legacies.
    - Challenges in healthcare access and quality.
    - Principle 7: Building Resilient Economies and Universal Healthcare.
9. **Regional Integration, Technological Advancement, and Climate Action**
    - Importance of regional cooperation and technology.
    - Addressing challenges for collective growth.
    - Harnessing renewable energy potential.
    - Principle 8: Fostering Regional Integration, Technology, and Sustainability.
10. **Enhancing Agricultural Productivity, Water Access, and Youth Empowerment**
    - Modernizing agricultural practices and value chains.
    - Addressing water scarcity and sanitation.
    - Fostering youth entrepreneurship and employment.

  - Principle 9: Agro-industrialization, Water Management, and Youth Development.
11. **Cultural Heritage, Quality Healthcare, and Urbanization**
  - Economic potential of Africa's cultural heritage.
  - Investing in healthcare and education.
  - Managing urbanization and promoting smart cities.
  - Principle 10: Cultural Tourism, Human Capital, and Sustainable Urbanization.
12. **Public-Private Partnerships, Innovation, and Governance**
  - Collaborative approaches to development.
  - Fostering innovation ecosystems.
  - Ensuring fair legal systems and governance.
  - Principle 11: Partnerships, Research, and Democratic Governance.
13. **Conclusion**
  - Summarizing key findings and encouraging collective efforts.
  - Vision for Africa's economic future.

RICH BUT POOR

Pethias Katampi

Introduction

The African continent, a land of captivating landscapes, diverse cultures, and storied history, has long captivated the world's imagination. From its breathtaking natural beauty to its rich tapestry of traditions, Africa is a realm of contrasts and complexities. It is within this dynamic backdrop that we embark on a profound exploration—the journey of unraveling the paradoxes that define its economic narrative in "Rich but Poor."

Setting the Stage: Africa's Wealth and Paradox

Amidst the splendor of Africa's abundant resources lies a haunting paradox—an enigma that has puzzled scholars, policymakers, and observers for generations. It is a paradox that hinges on the coexistence of immense resource wealth and enduring poverty. For centuries, Africa's riches have beckoned to explorers, entrepreneurs, and empires alike. Its treasure trove spans from the vast mineral reserves of diamond mines to the fertile plains yielding a bounty of crops. The allure of renewable energy resources, too, offers the promise of powering not only Africa's ambitions but also the world's future.

The African Natural Resource Landscape

The stage is set against a backdrop of unparalleled natural wealth. Africa's mineral wealth, beneath the surface and hidden within its rugged terrains, comprises the backbone of global industries. Precious metals, gems, and hydrocarbon resources have been coveted for their economic potential. The agricultural tapestry stretches far and wide, nourishing societies and serving as a testament to human ingenuity. Yet, these resources are a double-edged sword—a potential source of prosperity and yet a source of profound challenges.

Challenges and Opportunities of Resource Management

Harnessing the potential of Africa's resources requires a delicate balance—a balance between exploitation and stewardship. The road to sustainable development is fraught with challenges: how to extract minerals without harming the environment, how to cultivate the land without exhausting its fertility, and how to utilize renewable energy without compromising ecosystems. Each step forward necessitates prudent management, transparent governance, and equitable distribution—a call echoed in the principle of Responsible Resource Management for Equitable Development.

The Paradox of Abundance and Deprivation

In the shadows of this abundance stands a stark reality—a reality characterized by uneven development, poverty, and inequality. This paradox is the heart of Africa's economic narrative. The promise of prosperity often stands in contrast to the daily struggles of many. The legacy of historical injustices—rooted in colonization, the transatlantic slave trade, and internal conflicts—has cast a long shadow over the continent. The echoes of these past traumas resonate in the present, shaping the economic landscape and perpetuating cycles of deprivation.

A Vision for Prosperity: The Roadmap Ahead

As we navigate the pages of this book, we embark on a journey guided by principles that hold the promise of reshaping Africa's trajectory. These principles, firmly grounded in research and insights, provide a compass to navigate the complex economic landscape. From fostering social cohesion through interfaith dialogue to cultivating an ecosystem of innovation and research, each principle offers a piece of the puzzle—a vital step toward prosperity.

The chapters that follow explore these principles in depth, weaving together historical context, contemporary challenges, and aspirational visions. Each chapter invites you to delve into a realm of understanding, shedding light on the intricacies of Africa's economic narrative. Through the exploration of these principles, we hope to unearth pathways toward lasting transformation—a transformation that transcends the paradoxes and creates a tapestry of prosperity that stretches from the coastlines to the heartlands.

In a continent defined by resilience and a spirit of tenacity, the pursuit of prosperity is a collective endeavour—a journey that unfolds through cooperation, innovation, and the shared commitment to shaping a brighter future for all.

Chapter 2

African Natural Resources and Sustainable Development.

Overview of Africa's Natural Resources

Africa, a continent graced with diverse landscapes, is a realm of untold riches buried beneath its soil and spanning its horizons. These natural resources, lying beneath the earth's surface and adorning its fertile plains, hold the potential to shape Africa's destiny and radiate far beyond its borders.

Mineral Abundance: Precious Gems of the Earth

Africa's mineral wealth reads like a treasury of the earth's most sought-after treasures. The diamond mines of South Africa shimmer with tales of rarity and brilliance, while West Africa's gold fields whisper of prosperity that has spanned generations. The rich alluvial plains of the Congo Basin yield minerals like cobalt, essential for batteries that power our modern world. Namibia's vast deposits of uranium stand as a testament to the continent's nuclear potential. Copper, a versatile metal essential for construction and electronics, is abundant in the Democratic Republic of Congo, Zambia, and beyond.

Agricultural Bounty: Earth's Nourishing Gift

As the sun rises over Africa's vast savannahs and rainforests, a symphony of life emerges. These landscapes not only sustain diverse ecosystems but also hold the key to nourishing growing populations. The Nile Delta, historically known as the "breadbasket of the world," cultivates wheat and other crops that have sustained civilizations for millennia. Ethiopia's fertile highlands yield coffee, an elixir that has not only shaped local cultures but also the global palate. The palm groves of West Africa bear fruits like oil palm and coconut, essential ingredients for cooking, cosmetics, and more.

Renewable Energy: The Sunlit Path Forward

The sun, a constant companion in Africa's skies, is more than a celestial marvel—it's a source of limitless energy waiting to be harnessed. The Sahara Desert, known for its daunting heat, transforms into a goldmine of solar energy potential. Solar farms could sprawl across these arid landscapes, converting sunlight into electricity that could power entire cities. Wind currents whisper secrets of power along Africa's coastlines—wind farms tapping into the Atlantic and Indian Ocean breezes could send electricity coursing through grids. Rivers like the Congo, the Nile, and the Zambezi hold not only water but potential energy through hydropower.

Mineral, Agricultural, and Energy Nexus: Opportunity and Responsibility

As we peer deeper into the narrative of Africa's resources, we uncover not only promise but also responsibility. Responsible resource extraction, equitable distribution, and sustainable land management become essential tenets. The riches of minerals can't come at the cost of environmental degradation or social upheaval. Agricultural growth must be a dance between cultivating food and nurturing the earth's health. Renewable energy must be harnessed with respect for local communities and ecosystems.

Mapping the Future: A Path to Prosperity

In the pages ahead, we'll journey through the principles that underpin sustainable development, using these resources as touchpoints. From responsible management practices that safeguard ecosystems to equitable distribution that narrows the gap between rich and poor, each principle aligns with a vision where Africa's potential is harnessed for shared prosperity.

As we stand on the precipice of discovery, we invite you to explore the intricate tapestry of Africa's natural resources. These resources, like puzzle pieces, fit together to paint a portrait of possibility—one where wealth and responsibility interweave to create a legacy of enduring progress. From the diamonds that sparkle beneath the earth to the sunlight that bathes the land, Africa's resources beckon us toward a future where abundance enriches lives, empowers communities, and resonates across generations.

Challenges in Sustainable Resource Management

As Africa's diverse landscapes reveal the allure of its natural resources, a complex tapestry of challenges emerges in the quest for responsible and sustainable management. The riches embedded within the earth's crust, the fertile plains, and the renewable energy potential beckon progress, yet navigating these treasures requires overcoming multifaceted obstacles that span environmental, social, and economic dimensions.

Environmental Degradation: Balancing Prosperity and Preservation

Resource extraction, while offering a path to economic prosperity, often exacts an environmental toll. The allure of mineral wealth has led to deforestation, habitat destruction, and water pollution. The excavation of minerals, if unchecked, can scar landscapes and disrupt ecosystems, causing long-lasting ecological imbalances. Striking the delicate equilibrium between harnessing resources and safeguarding the environment stands as a pivotal challenge in sustainable resource management.

Land Use Conflicts: The Dilemma of Development

African lands teem with potential: beneath them lie mineral veins while above them, fertile fields beckon agricultural development. Yet, harmonizing these dual roles often sparks conflicts. The tension between mining operations and local communities dependent on the land for farming, grazing, and cultural practices is a complex puzzle. Effective land use strategies must accommodate diverse needs, ensuring that resource extraction coexists with community well-being and ecological health.

Resource Governance and Corruption: Bridging Transparency and Fairness

Sustainable development hinges on transparent and accountable governance of resources. Yet, this arena is marred by challenges such as corruption and mismanagement. When resource revenues are diverted away from public welfare, corruption flourishes, and equitable development falters. Building robust governance frameworks that ensure the benefits of resource extraction reach those who need them most is essential to circumvent this challenge.

Infrastructure and Technology Gaps: Building Bridges to Sustainability

The responsible management of resources requires robust infrastructure and cutting-edge technology. Insufficient transportation networks can amplify environmental impacts by hindering efficient resource transport. Moreover, the absence of technology and expertise can impede the adoption of eco-friendly practices, exacerbating the challenges of sustainability. Bridging these gaps is vital for the responsible management of resources.

Social Displacement and Inequalities: The Human Side of Extraction

Resource extraction ventures can unintentionally unravel the social fabric of communities. The relocation of people from their ancestral lands, often driven by mining or energy projects, leads to displacement and the loss of cultural heritage. Moreover, these challenges intersect with broader socioeconomic inequalities, as the benefits of resource extraction may not reach those most in need. Addressing these inequalities becomes imperative for sustainable resource management.

Conflict and Security Concerns: Navigating Fragile Ground

History underscores that natural resources can ignite conflicts, both within and beyond borders. Competing interests in valuable resources can escalate tensions, leading to local disputes or even regional conflicts. The potential for conflicts to erupt around valuable resources emphasizes the need for effective governance mechanisms to prevent resource-driven disputes.

Global Market Volatility: Surfing the Waves of Economic Shifts

Africa's economies, often dependent on resource exports, are susceptible to global market fluctuations. The volatility of commodity prices, whether in minerals or agricultural products, can send shockwaves through national economies. These fluctuations can disrupt long-term development plans and reveal the vulnerability of economies reliant on a single revenue stream.

Charting a Sustainable Course: Tackling Challenges with Resolve

While the challenges in sustainable resource management are formidable, they offer a canvas upon which Africa's transformation can be painted. Recognizing and addressing these obstacles is the first step toward responsible stewardship. The principles that underpin responsible resource management serve as guideposts, directing efforts toward strategies that harmonize economic advancement with ecological preservation, social equity, and a legacy of prosperity for generations to come.

Principle 1: Responsible Resource Management for Equitable Development

Safeguarding Environmental Integrity: A Promise to the Earth

In the pursuit of equitable development, responsible resource management stands as a promise to the earth itself. The preservation of fragile ecosystems, the protection of biodiversity, and the prevention of irreversible damage are at the heart of this commitment. The extraction of minerals must be approached with strategies that minimize ecological disruption, allowing the landscapes to heal and thrive alongside human progress.

Transparency and Equitable Distribution: A Path to Fairness

Transparency and equitable distribution are the bedrock upon which responsible resource management is built. Ensuring that the wealth generated from resource extraction reaches all segments of society—rather than being confined to the corridors of power—is a key element of this principle. By channelling revenues into education, healthcare, infrastructure, and social welfare, nations can address historical inequalities and pave the way for a more balanced and just future.

Empowering Local Communities: A Symphony of Voices

Local communities living in the shadows of resource-rich lands are not mere bystanders; they are stakeholders whose lives intertwine with the fate of these resources. Empowering these communities to participate in decision-making processes is paramount. This involvement not only ensures their perspectives are considered but also fosters a sense of ownership and guardianship. Sustainable development that Honors both indigenous knowledge and modern progress emerges from these collaborations.

Technology and Innovation: A Vision for Progress

Technology and innovation hold the key to responsible resource management. Innovations in mining techniques can minimize environmental impact, from the use of eco-friendly chemicals to advanced drilling methods. Precision agriculture, driven by technological advancements, optimizes land use, minimizes water consumption, and maximizes crop yields. Sustainable energy technologies, too, are indispensable, ensuring that power generation aligns with environmental preservation.

Striking a Balance: Navigating Challenges and Seizing Opportunities

Navigating the principle of responsible resource management is a dance between challenges and opportunities. The delicate balance between economic growth and environmental preservation requires a collaborative effort by governments, industries, communities, and global partners. This principle calls for harmonious integration of diverse perspectives, recognizing that wealth creation from the earth's resources must be matched by a commitment to stewardship.

A Future of Promise: Responsible Prosperity

The principle of Responsible Resource Management for Equitable Development is a testament to the continent's determination to weave a future of responsible prosperity. It sets forth a vision where prosperity is not confined to minerals or energy, but where it resonates through the lives of those who call Africa home. This principle, embraced by governments, embraced by industries, embraced by communities, paves a path toward a legacy where the treasures of the earth are not depleted but renewed—a future that shines with promise for Africa and the world.

Chapter 3

Religion, Social Harmony, and Inclusive Growth

Historical and Cultural Role of Religion in Africa

A Tapestry of Beliefs: The Rich Mosaic of African Religions

Africa's cultural landscape is a mesmerizing tapestry intricately woven with a myriad of belief systems, each contributing to the breathtaking mosaic of spirituality. From the towering pyramids of ancient Egypt to the sacred groves tucked away in the heart of sub-Saharan communities, religion has been an immutable aspect of African societies for centuries. These belief systems are not mere conduits to the divine; they are living repositories of history, wisdom, and identity, forming an essential part of the cultural fabric that defines the continent.

The Power of Ancestral Spirits: A Bridge to the Past

Ancestor veneration stands as a common thread that unites many African religions, acting as a conduit that bridges the gap between the living and the departed. The spirits of ancestors are held in reverence as guiding lights, protectors, and bestowers of blessings upon their descendants. This deep-seated reverence serves as a channel for preserving a sense of continuity, a spiritual lifeline that connects present generations to the ancient roots of their lineage. Beyond being individual guides, ancestral spirits also hold a communal role—mediators in disputes, custodians of communal harmony, and reminders of the shared history that unites communities.

Rituals and Ceremonies: Expressions of Identity and Unity

Religious rituals and ceremonies are far more than scripted performances; they are profound expressions of identity and unity. These rites constitute a spectrum of human experience, marking pivotal moments in the individual and collective journey. From elaborate initiation ceremonies that signify transitions from childhood to adulthood to the joyous celebrations of harvest and the changing seasons, these rituals serve as sacred expressions of cultural identity. More than that, they encapsulate the spirit of unity, reinforcing the bonds that connect individuals and communities through shared experiences. Music, dance, and art woven into these rituals not only elevate their significance but also solidify their place in the cultural legacy.

Adaptation and Syncretism: The Resilience of African Religions

The evolution of African religions stands as a testament to the continent's remarkable resilience and adaptability. Africa's history is a tapestry woven with threads of encounters—encounters with foreign cultures through trade, migration, and colonization. These interactions have led to a phenomenon known as syncretism, where indigenous beliefs meld with the doctrines of imported faiths. Christianity, Islam, and other religious traditions have woven themselves into the fabric of Africa's cultural landscape, resulting in unique expressions of spirituality that bear the imprints of diverse influences. This adaptive spirit showcases the dynamic nature of African religions, where ancient traditions integrate with the currents of change while maintaining their core essence.

Beyond Borders: Religion's Influence on Society

Religion in Africa transcends the realm of individual belief; it extends its reach into the very fabric of societal structures and dynamics.

Spiritual leaders often serve as mediators in conflicts, lending their wisdom to promote peace, reconciliation, and harmony. Religious institutions assume roles that stretch beyond spiritual guidance, transforming into platforms for education, healthcare, and community development. In regions where state services may fall short, religious institutions step in to bridge the gaps. By contributing to education, health, and social welfare, these institutions play a pivotal role in nurturing societies that are not only spiritually rich but also socially empowered.

Unity in Diversity: Fostering Inclusive Growth

The historical and cultural significance of religion in Africa embodies the potential for fostering inclusive growth. Beneath the mosaic of diverse belief systems lies a common thread of shared values and ethics that traverse linguistic, ethnic, and geographical boundaries. These shared values—compassion, justice, and communal well-being—provide a fertile ground for fostering an environment of inclusivity. Leveraging these values, societies can foster an atmosphere where each individual's potential is unlocked and every community member contributes to and benefits from the fruits of progress.

Religious practices and their effects on society

False Prophets and Distorted Teachings: A New Era of Worship

The evolution of religion in Africa has given rise to a distinctive phenomenon—the surge of charismatic leaders known as "false prophets." These individuals, often charismatic and persuasive, command substantial followings with their captivating preaching styles and purported miracles. While these charismatic leaders have garnered large followings, their practices have at times strayed from the foundational teachings of their respective religions, giving rise to discussions on the broader impact on social harmony, inclusive growth, and poverty within African societies.

Examining the New Style of Worship: A Defiance of Teachings

Central to the concerns surrounding these false prophets is the way they challenge established religious teachings. Particularly, the practice of addressing these leaders as "Papa" or "Daddy" raises theological questions. Matthew 23:9, a foundational scripture, cautions against using such titles of reverence, emphasizing that "And do not call anyone on earth your father; for One is your Father, He who is in heaven." This directive underscores the principle of equality and humility, promoting a sense of shared fraternity among believers.

Distortion of Teachings: A Critical Examination

A deeper exploration of Matthew 23 uncovers the context in which Jesus warned against pursuing elevated positions within religious institutions. The passage criticizes individuals who seek titles of authority and take pleasure in being addressed as "teachers" or "fathers." The critique targets the hubris that seeks self-glorification, which contrasts with the humble and compassionate teachings of Jesus. Distinct from honouring biological parents, as emphasized in Exodus 20:12, this rebuke cautions against adopting grandiose titles within religious contexts.

The True Measure of Authenticity: "You Will Know Them by Their Fruits"

The teachings of Matthew 7:21 add a profound layer to the discourse on authenticity. Jesus' words, "Not everyone who says to Me, 'Lord, Lord,' shall enter the kingdom of heaven, but he who does the will of My Father in heaven," highlights the significance of actions over words. This teaching underlines that genuine faith is manifested through deeds and adherence to divine principles. Jesus warns of those who may perform extraordinary acts, even casting out demons, yet lack alignment with divine values. The declaration, "I never knew you; depart from Me," underscores the necessity for authentic and transformative faith.

The Peril of Ignorance: "My People Perish for Lack of Knowledge"

The scripture from Hosea 4:6, "My people perish for lack of knowledge," serves as a poignant reminder of the crucial role of seeking knowledge and understanding. This verse accentuates the vulnerability that arises when individuals prioritize external pronouncements over personal exploration of truth. The allure of charismatic leaders and the spectacle of supposed miracles can overshadow the value of studying religious texts and nurturing a deeper relationship with faith. This scriptural wisdom calls for proactive knowledge-seeking, resisting the lure of being swayed solely by external proclamations.

The Erosion of Authenticity: The Search for Miracles

The pursuit of miracles, often extolled by false prophets, can divert attention from the core tenets of faith. This quest for immediate, extraordinary interventions can diminish the significance of ethical living, compassion, and humility. In contrast to the teachings of Jesus, which prioritize faith, compassion, and ethical conduct, the fixation on materialistic and miraculous displays can distort the essence of spirituality. This shift can lead individuals away from introspection, self-improvement, and personal transformation that genuine religious teachings advocate.

Impact on Social Harmony and Inclusive Growth

The rise of false prophets has raised concerns about the potential erosion of social harmony. Their persuasive influence and unconventional practices can create divisions along religious lines and exacerbate tensions among believers. Additionally, their materialistic tendencies, evident in their lavish lifestyles and extravagant possessions, have led to accusations of exploiting vulnerable individuals seeking spiritual guidance. The traditional teachings of social justice, humility, and compassion often championed by established religious authorities can be overshadowed by the commercialization of faith.

Poverty and the Commercialization of Faith: A Troubling Confluence

The practices of these false prophets have tangible implications for poverty within African societies. The opulent displays of wealth by these leaders contrast starkly with the financial struggles endured by many of their followers. The misallocation of resources—often channelled into lavish donations, tithes, and offerings—can exacerbate poverty by diverting crucial funds away from basic necessities towards religious institutions. The pressure to contribute generously to these leaders, under the promise of prosperity, can plunge individuals deeper into financial hardship, perpetuating a cycle of impoverishment.

Divergence from True Values: An Economic Consequence

The diversion of resources toward the opulent lifestyles of false prophets creates an economic divide that directly impacts poverty rates. The elevation of materialism above the core tenets of compassion, empathy, and societal well-being detracts from efforts to uplift marginalized communities. Traditional religious teachings often underscored supporting the needy, widows, and orphans. However, the commercialized approach embraced by false prophets shifts the emphasis towards personal enrichment, creating a jarring discord between spiritual teachings and economic realities.

A Call for Ethical Stewardship

The emergence of false prophets and their alignment with materialism underscores the pressing need for ethical stewardship within faith communities. The essence of religious teachings, be it Christianity or any other faith, remains grounded in values that prioritize social harmony, compassion, and inclusivity. Realigning religious practices with these principles and resisting the allure of distorted interpretations can empower African societies to break free from the clutches of poverty perpetuated by misguided spiritual leaders.

Principle 2: Promoting Tolerance and Interfaith Dialogue for Social Development

Religion as a Unifying and Divisive Force

Religion has long held a profound influence on societies, shaping cultural norms, moral values, and worldviews. In Africa, where diverse religious traditions coexist, religion possesses the power to both unite and divide communities. While religious practices often foster a sense of belonging and purpose, they can also become sources of tension when different faiths intersect. Thus, embracing the principle of promoting tolerance and interfaith dialogue is vital for cultivating social development and fostering peaceful coexistence.

Tolerance: A Pillar of Harmonious Societies

Tolerance is the cornerstone of harmonious societies, facilitating the coexistence of diverse religious, ethnic, and cultural groups. It signifies not merely a passive acceptance of differences, but an active embrace of diversity. Tolerance encourages individuals to engage in open-minded conversations, respecting differing viewpoints without vilifying or alienating others. This principle underscores that unity is not synonymous with uniformity; instead, it thrives on the rich tapestry of perspectives and beliefs.

Interfaith Dialogue: Bridging Divides

Interfaith dialogue emerges as a powerful tool to bridge divides and nurture understanding among adherents of different faiths. Such dialogues provide a platform for individuals to share their beliefs, practices, and experiences, promoting empathy and dispelling misconceptions. Through these exchanges, common values and shared aspirations often come to light, emphasizing the universal human quest for purpose, compassion, and community.

The Economic and Social Benefits of Interfaith Harmony

Promoting tolerance and interfaith dialogue yields far-reaching economic and social benefits. By mitigating religious tensions, societies create an environment conducive to innovation, collaboration, and collective progress. Cooperation among diverse groups can lead to the pooling of resources, knowledge, and expertise, resulting in economic growth and improved living standards. Furthermore, interfaith harmony nurtures a sense of belonging, reducing social isolation and fostering the collective well-being of all members.

Addressing Root Causes of Division

The principle of tolerance and interfaith dialogue encourages societies to address the underlying factors contributing to division. Often, prejudices and biases stem from a lack of exposure and understanding. By actively engaging in conversations and seeking to learn about one another, individuals can challenge preconceived notions and dismantle stereotypes. This process not only fosters religious harmony but also paves the way for a more inclusive, accepting, and united society.

Promoting Education and Awareness

Promoting tolerance and interfaith dialogue begins with education and awareness. Schools, religious institutions, and community centers play pivotal roles in fostering an environment that encourages open-mindedness and respect for differences. Incorporating interfaith studies into curricula can empower the younger generation with the tools to embrace diversity and challenge discriminatory attitudes. Additionally, encouraging religious leaders to engage in interfaith dialogue sets a positive example and amplifies the message of unity.

The Role of Government and Civil Society

Governments and civil society organizations also play instrumental roles in promoting tolerance and interfaith dialogue. Policies that protect religious freedoms and discourage discrimination create an inclusive atmosphere for diverse faith communities. Establishing platforms for interfaith gatherings, workshops, and seminars fosters meaningful exchanges that ripple through communities. By prioritizing diversity and actively seeking collaboration, societies can cultivate a sense of shared responsibility for social development.

This encapsulates the essence of nurturing social development by fostering tolerance and interfaith dialogue. As African societies continue to navigate the intricacies of religious diversity, embracing this principle can lead to improved social cohesion, economic advancement, and harmonious coexistence. By acknowledging the richness of cultural and religious differences and seeking common ground, individuals and communities lay the foundation for a brighter and more inclusive future.

Chapter 4

Governance, Corruption, and Effective Resource Allocation

In a pursuit to decipher Africa's enigma of bountiful natural resources juxtaposed with enduring poverty, Chapter 4 of "Rich but Poor" embarks on a voyage through the intricate realm of governance, corruption, and resource allocation. Within these pages, the labyrinthine corridors of power are navigated to expose how corruption, mismanagement, and a dearth of transparency erode the foundation of equitable progress across the continent. This chapter further delves into the reverberations of such practices, shedding light on their adverse impacts on poverty and economic advancement.

Unveiling the Grasp of Corruption

As the chapter's narrative unfurls, a stark reality emerges — the pervasive grip of corruption within the governance frameworks of numerous African nations. This insidious phenomenon stifles the efficient allocation of resources, distorts the equitable distribution of wealth, and sabotages endeavors aimed at uplifting marginalized communities. The exploration of this topic unveils the intricate interplay between corruption and the continent's developmental challenges.

It's not merely about the skewed allocation of resources; corruption's tendrils extend to weaken essential public services, including education, healthcare, and infrastructure development. Through gripping narratives and poignant case studies, this section unveils how corrupt practices intertwine with the perpetuation of poverty, ensnaring countless African citizens within cycles of deprivation and despair.

Greedy Leadership and Its Impact

Central to the discussion on governance and corruption lies the issue of greedy leadership, a factor that has profoundly impacted African societies. The prevalence of leaders prioritizing personal gain over the well-being of their citizens has exacerbated the challenges of corruption and poverty. This avaricious pursuit of wealth and power by those in positions of authority has had far-reaching consequences, leaving a trail of devastation in its wake.

Zambia's Corruption Quagmire

A pertinent case study emerges in Zambia, where instances of corruption have ensnared the nation's aspirations for progress. The misappropriation of funds, controversial procurements, and mismanagement of resources have left the country grappling with poverty despite its vast mineral wealth. The case of the 42 fire trucks purchased at an exorbitant cost of $42 million vividly illustrates how corruption diverts funds away from essential services, exacerbating the challenges of poverty eradication.

THE BLEAK CONSEQUENCES

Greedy leadership, driven by self-interest and avarice, has resulted in skewed policies that favor the elite while neglecting the needs of the majority. This has led to rampant inequality, where a small fraction of the population accumulates immense wealth while the rest struggle to access basic services. The very institutions that should be protecting the interests of the people have been co-opted to serve the interests of a select few, deepening the cycle of poverty.

Erosion of Trust and Civic Participation

The erosion of trust in leadership due to greed has hindered civic participation and democratic processes. When citizens perceive that their leaders are primarily concerned with personal gain, they become disillusioned with the political system. This disillusionment can lead to apathy, reducing the active engagement of citizens in shaping their own destinies. Thus, the potential for a collective effort to demand accountability and transparency is stifled.

Hindrance to Development

Greedy leadership often results in misallocation of resources, as funds that should be invested in critical sectors like education, healthcare, and infrastructure are diverted for personal gain. This misallocation obstructs the potential for sustainable development, leaving nations grappling with underdeveloped infrastructure and inadequately equipped citizens.

Reinforcing Corruption

The presence of greedy leaders creates an environment ripe for corruption to flourish. Leaders more interested in personal enrichment than in public welfare often turn a blind eye to corrupt practices within their administrations. This lack of commitment to accountability and transparency perpetuates a culture of corruption, further draining resources that could otherwise be used to uplift communities.

Struggle for Accountability

Within African societies, an ongoing battle against corruption is fought on multiple fronts. This section delves into the resilience of activists, civil society organizations, and independent media, who tirelessly champion transparency and good governance. These individuals and groups emerge as beacons of change, playing a pivotal role in exposing corruption, advocating for transformation, and holding leaders accountable for their actions.

its essence is encapsulated in the call for transparency, accountability, and good governance as the cornerstones for eradicating poverty. The imperative for comprehensive strategies reverberates — strategies that don't just expose corruption but prioritize the equitable distribution of resources to uplift marginalized communities.

Reflections and Beyond

Through the lens of governance, corruption, and resource allocation, Chapter 4 lays bare Africa's challenges. Yet, it also unveils an opportunity for transformation, a chance for the continent to reshape its trajectory. As "Rich but Poor" unfolds, it presents a roadmap towards a future where transparent governance dismantles the chains of corruption, paving the way for equitable prosperity across the vast African landscape.

Principle 3: Championing Transparent and Accountable Governance

Embedded within this chapter is Principle 3 — Transparent and Accountable Governance — an imperative that stands as a beacon of hope. Transparent decision-making processes, coupled with mechanisms for oversight, form the bedrock of equitable resource allocation. The significance of this principle echoes as the antidote to corruption's corrosive effects, shaping the narrative towards a brighter future.

Chapter 5

Historical Injustices and Internal Conflicts

Historical Context of the Transatlantic Slave Trade and Colonization

Within the annals of Africa's complex economic story lies a chapter marked by historical injustices and internal conflicts, deeply rooted in the historical context of the transatlantic slave trade and colonization. These epochs have left an indelible mark on the continent's fabric, shaping its economic landscape and social dynamics in profound ways.

The Transatlantic Slave Trade, a somber period that spanned centuries, remains an irrevocable scar on Africa's history. This transcontinental commerce in human lives forcibly displaced millions from their homes, tearing apart families and communities while enriching foreign powers. The economies of European nations flourished at the expense of African dignity, culture, and human potential. The echoes of this trade continue to reverberate through time, influencing the socio-economic disparities that persist today.

Colonization further exacerbated Africa's plight. European powers carved up the continent, setting artificial borders that often ignored existing cultural, linguistic, and ethnic ties. This colonial scramble led to the creation of nations arbitrarily divided, sowing the seeds of internal conflicts that continue to challenge unity and cooperation. The scramble for Africa's resources - minerals, land, and labor - fueled the economic engines of the colonizers, leaving the indigenous populations to grapple with economic exploitation and cultural erasure.

The legacy of colonization lingers as a testament to Africa's enduring resilience. The economic structures that emerged during this era continue to shape patterns of resource extraction, trade, and wealth distribution. The exploitation of Africa's wealth for the benefit of foreign powers has perpetuated cycles of poverty, inequality, and economic dependency.

The scars of historical injustices and internal conflicts have not healed easily. The legacy of the transatlantic slave trade and colonization has left deep socio-economic divides, which in turn have fueled tensions and struggles within African societies. These internal conflicts are often rooted in historical grievances, unequal access to resources, and disparities in economic opportunities.

However, amidst this complexity, there is a glimmer of hope. Many African nations are actively working to address these historical injustices, seeking ways to heal wounds, foster unity, and promote inclusivity. The acknowledgment of past wrongs serves as a foundation for reconciliation and growth, as societies strive to build bridges across ethnic, cultural, and historical divisions.

As Africa confronts the shadows of its history, the continent's journey toward economic liberation gains a new dimension. By understanding the historical context of the transatlantic slave trade and colonization, Africa's nations can better navigate the intricate path of development. Acknowledging these injustices is a step toward building a more equitable future, where the lessons of history are harnessed to forge unity, cooperation, and a shared economic prosperity.

In the intricate tapestry of Africa's past, the historical context of the transatlantic slave trade and colonization is a thread that weaves together the challenges and possibilities of the present. As Africa stands at the crossroads of its economic destiny, the resilience of its people and their commitment to a brighter future provide the guiding light toward a more just and prosperous continent.

African Involvement in the Slave Trade and Consequences

The historical narrative of Africa's involvement in the transatlantic slave trade reveals a complex and multifaceted tale that has left enduring consequences on the continent's socio-economic fabric. Acknowledging this facet of history is essential for understanding the broader context of Africa's economic challenges and aspirations.

While the transatlantic slave trade was predominantly orchestrated by European colonial powers, it's crucial to recognize that African societies were not mere passive victims in this trade. Many African rulers and societies were entangled in the slave trade as participants, suppliers, or intermediaries. This painful collaboration, driven by political rivalries and economic incentives, complicated the ethical and moral landscape of the trade.

A sobering aspect to consider is that Africans, at times, played a role in selling their fellow brothers and sisters to other races. This grim reality is an indication that historical dynamics were complex and motivated by various factors, including power struggles, economic gain, and societal divisions. It serves as a reminder that historical events are rarely black and white, and the transatlantic slave trade was marked by intricate webs of complicity and exploitation.

The consequences of Africa's involvement in the slave trade were multifaceted and profound. The forcible extraction of millions of men, women, and children from their homes resulted in immense human suffering, fracturing families and communities. The social and demographic impact was staggering, disrupting the continuity of cultural practices, traditions, and knowledge transfer.

Economically, the slave trade disrupted local economies and labor dynamics. It led to the diversion of human resources away from agriculture, handicrafts, and other productive sectors, crippling the potential for autonomous economic growth. The wealth accumulated from the trade did not trickle down to benefit African societies at large; instead, it further enriched a select few, often exacerbating existing power imbalances.

The consequences of the transatlantic slave trade also extended beyond the era of its direct operations. The legacy of slavery continues to shape African societies and their relationships with the global economy. The trauma and loss experienced during this period have left lasting scars, influencing social norms, cultural perceptions, and economic opportunities for generations.

However, it's crucial to emphasize that Africa's involvement in the slave trade does not define the continent's history or potential. Just as the transatlantic slave trade was a complex and multifaceted phenomenon, so too is Africa's path toward economic liberation. The continent's history encompasses both pain and resilience, and acknowledging this complexity is an essential step toward achieving a more equitable and prosperous future.

Africans have drawn strength from their history to address the lingering consequences of the slave trade. From community efforts to heal intergenerational wounds to broader initiatives aimed at promoting education, cultural preservation, and economic empowerment, Africa's response to its past is marked by determination and resilience.

As Africa navigates the road ahead, understanding the consequences of its involvement in the transatlantic slave trade adds depth and nuance to its pursuit of economic liberation. By confronting the complexities of history and the enduring impact of the past, African nations can chart a course toward a future characterized by unity, cooperation, and inclusive growth. The continent's progress hinges on recognizing the lessons of history while forging ahead with determination, resilience, and a shared commitment to building a more just and prosperous society.

Analysing Internal Conflicts and Their Toll

Throughout Africa's history, internal conflicts have played a significant role in shaping the trajectory of the continent's development. These conflicts, often rooted in ethnic, religious, political, and economic tensions, have exacted a heavy toll on African societies, exacerbating poverty and hindering progress. Analyzing the nature and impact of internal conflicts is essential for understanding the challenges Africa faces in achieving economic prosperity and social harmony.

Internal conflicts in Africa have been diverse in their causes and manifestations. Some conflicts have been driven by ethnic rivalries, as different ethnic groups vie for political power, control over resources, or recognition. Others have been fueled by political instability, as power struggles and governance issues lead to unrest and violence. Religious and ideological differences have also contributed to conflict, with tensions arising from differing worldviews and beliefs.

The toll of internal conflicts on Africa has been profound, affecting various dimensions of development:

1. **Humanitarian Crisis:** Internal conflicts often result in mass displacement of populations, leading to refugee crises and internal displacement. Civilians are forced to flee their

homes, leaving behind their livelihoods and sources of income. The loss of homes, access to basic services, and social cohesion disrupts the normal functioning of communities.

2. **Economic Disruption:** Conflict disrupts economic activities, causing a decline in productivity, trade, and investment. Infrastructure, including roads, schools, and healthcare facilities, is often damaged or destroyed, hampering economic growth and development. The diversion of resources to conflict-related activities further strains national budgets and limits investment in critical sectors.
3. **Social Cohesion:** Internal conflicts strain the social fabric of societies, often pitting different groups against each other. Divisions along ethnic, religious, or political lines can result in long-lasting animosities that impede efforts toward unity and cooperation. The breakdown of trust hinders social progress and inclusivity.
4. **Education and Human Capital:** Conflict disrupts education systems, preventing children and youth from accessing quality education. Disrupted education hampers human capital development, limiting the potential for economic growth and innovation.
5. **Healthcare and Development:** Conflict-ridden regions often face challenges in healthcare access and delivery. Displacement, disrupted healthcare systems, and reduced access to essential services contribute to increased disease prevalence and hinder overall development.
6. **Gender Inequality:** Women and girls are disproportionately affected by internal conflicts. They often face heightened risks of sexual and gender-based violence, trafficking, and exploitation. Conflict-related displacement and disruption of social services can exacerbate gender inequalities.

7. **Political Instability:** Internal conflicts can undermine democratic governance and political stability. Fragile institutions and governance structures can result in prolonged political crises and lack of effective leadership.

The complexities of internal conflicts in Africa also extend to issues such as violence within communities. For instance, examining incidents of violence among individuals from the same racial or ethnic background, commonly referred to as "black on black" violence, highlights a complex dynamic influenced by historical, social, and economic factors. Such violence, while not unique to Africa, underscores the urgent need for holistic solutions that address root causes and promote community safety.

Efforts to address internal conflicts in Africa require a multi-faceted approach that addresses both the immediate humanitarian needs and the underlying drivers of conflict. Sustainable peace and stability demand investments in conflict prevention, resolution, and post-conflict reconstruction. This includes promoting inclusive political processes, building effective institutions, and fostering social cohesion.

The path to economic liberation in Africa necessitates not only addressing the legacy of historical injustices but also tackling the contemporary challenges of internal conflicts. By investing in conflict resolution, peacebuilding, and inclusive governance, African nations can create an environment conducive to economic growth, social harmony, and the fulfillment of their people's potential. Ultimately, the transformation of historical conflict into cooperative progress can pave the way for a brighter future for Africa and its citizens.

In reflecting on the historical injustices and internal conflicts that have shaped Africa's trajectory, it becomes clear that these elements are among the many reasons for the persistence of poverty on the continent. The intricate web of conflicts, stemming from historical injustices, ethnic rivalries, political struggles, and economic disparities, has hindered progress and stifled the potential for collective growth.

Perhaps one of the most striking realizations is that unity and a collective sense of responsibility have often been lacking. The history of internal conflicts, divisions, and even instances of Africans participating in the transatlantic slave trade reveal a complex narrative of societal fragmentation. Instead of working together to overcome challenges, there have been instances where self-interest has taken precedence over the common good.

It is undeniable that true transformation demands a shift in perspective, one that places unity and collective well-being at the forefront. A continent rich in cultural diversity, resources, and human capital has the potential to achieve remarkable growth and prosperity if its people come together. Breaking the cycle of internal conflicts and historical injustices requires a commitment to inclusivity, respect for diverse perspectives, and a shared vision of progress.

As we confront the legacy of internal conflicts and the fractures they have wrought, let us recognize that Africa's liberation from poverty demands a unified effort. We must strive to build bridges of understanding and empathy, focusing on collaborative solutions that transcend individual gains. By embracing a spirit of solidarity and cooperation, Africans can harness their rich potential and pave the way for a future where the continent's wealth benefits all its people. The journey toward equitable prosperity is not without its challenges, but with a united front, Africa's narrative can evolve from one of division to one of collective achievement and shared success.

Principle 4: Fostering Unity, Cooperation, and Inclusive Societies.

The principle of fostering unity, cooperation, and inclusive societies stands as a guiding beacon for Africa's journey towards equitable development. It encapsulates the recognition that the challenges faced by the continent cannot be addressed in isolation. Instead, they require a collective effort that transcends borders, ethnicities, and historical divisions. This principle underscores the essential truth that a united Africa is a stronger Africa – one that can harness its immense potential and overcome the obstacles that have hindered progress for far too long.

Historical injustices, rooted in the transatlantic slave trade and colonization, have left deep scars across Africa. These wounds are not only historical but have reverberated through generations, influencing societal dynamics, perceptions, and interactions. To move forward, Africa must confront its past and acknowledge the painful realities it holds. By doing so, the continent can begin the healing process, mend fractured identities, and pave the way for a united front against the challenges that persist.

A critical aspect of this principle is acknowledging the role that Africans themselves played in the transatlantic slave trade. While external forces were undoubtedly responsible for initiating and perpetuating this cruel system, it is an uncomfortable truth that some Africans participated in the capturing and selling of their fellow brothers and sisters. This painful history is a reminder of the complex interplay between external manipulation and internal divisions. It highlights the urgent need for Africans to recognize their shared humanity and to work towards a future where unity prevails over division.

Internal conflicts, fueled by various factors including ethnic, religious, and political differences, have also taken a toll on Africa's progress. The consequences of such conflicts are devastating, leading to loss of life, displacement, and the erosion of social cohesion. By embracing the principle of fostering unity and cooperation, African nations can channel their energy towards addressing shared challenges rather than being consumed by internal strife.

Inclusive societies are at the heart of this principle. Inclusivity demands that all members of society, regardless of their background, have an equal opportunity to contribute to and benefit from the continent's growth. This requires policies that address disparities in education, employment, and access to resources. It also calls for an end to the violence that has plagued African communities and an increased commitment to dialogue and reconciliation.

Fostering unity, cooperation, and inclusive societies is not a simple task, but it is a transformative one. It requires a collective shift in mindset – a move away from narrow self-interest towards a broader vision of shared prosperity. By embracing this principle, Africa can break free from the chains of division and forge a future where its rich resources are harnessed for the well-being of all its citizens. In doing so, the continent can transcend its history of exploitation and conflict, emerging as a beacon of cooperation, resilience, and hope.

Chapter 6

Empowering African Entrepreneurs and Businesses

Examining Systemic Barriers to Black Wealth Creation

Empowering African entrepreneurs and fostering a thriving business ecosystem is crucial in addressing Africa's paradox of natural resource wealth coexisting with widespread poverty. However, this goal is hampered by systemic barriers that have historically impeded the creation of black wealth and constrained the continent's economic progress.

Systemic barriers are deeply embedded challenges that hinder the advancement of black individuals and communities in the realm of entrepreneurship. These barriers encompass a range of obstacles, including historical injustices, limited access to financial resources, unequal educational opportunities, and discriminatory practices across industries. These factors combine to create a complex web of challenges for aspiring black entrepreneurs striving to establish and grow successful enterprises.

Historical injustices, such as colonization and slavery, continue to reverberate through Africa's socio-economic fabric. These injustices have contributed to persistent disparities in wealth and opportunity, making it arduous for black entrepreneurs to break free from cycles of poverty and limited access to resources. Moreover, securing adequate capital remains a significant challenge, as many black entrepreneurs face difficulties in obtaining funding to initiate or expand their businesses. Discriminatory lending practices and underrepresentation within financial institutions further exacerbate this issue.

Unequal access to quality education and relevant training compounds the hurdles faced by black entrepreneurs. Education plays a pivotal role in equipping individuals with the skills and knowledge necessary to navigate modern business environments. Yet, disparities in educational opportunities hinder the development of a skilled workforce capable of driving innovation and economic growth.

Overcoming these systemic barriers necessitates a multi-pronged approach that involves collaboration between governments, private sector entities, civil society organizations, and international partners. Initiatives aimed at promoting equitable access to capital, financial literacy programs, and targeted support for black entrepreneurs can contribute to a more level playing field. Furthermore, investing in education and skills development for marginalized communities is essential for nurturing a new generation of entrepreneurs equipped to thrive.

Empowering African entrepreneurs not only spurs economic growth but also dismantles the systemic barriers perpetuating inequality and impeding progress. By dismantling these barriers, Africa can harness the full potential of its entrepreneurial spirit, stimulating innovation, generating employment opportunities, and driving sustainable development. Embracing entrepreneurship as a catalyst for change requires a collective commitment to creating an environment where all individuals, regardless of their background, can actively participate in and reap the benefits of Africa's economic transformation.

Success Stories of African Entrepreneurs

Amidst the challenges and systemic barriers, Africa's entrepreneurial landscape also shines with inspiring success stories that exemplify the potential for black wealth creation and economic empowerment. These success stories showcase the resilience, innovation, and determination of African entrepreneurs who have defied the odds to build thriving businesses and contribute significantly to their communities and the continent as a whole.

These entrepreneurs have harnessed their unique skills, talents, and insights to identify opportunities and create value across various industries. They serve as beacons of hope, demonstrating that with the right support and conducive environments, African entrepreneurs can compete on a global scale and make lasting impacts. Their journeys reflect the transformative power of entrepreneurship in driving economic growth, creating jobs, and fostering social change.

One notable example is the story of Mo Ibrahim, a Sudanese-born entrepreneur who founded Celtel, a telecommunications company that brought affordable mobile services to millions of people across Africa. His vision of connecting the unconnected not only revolutionized communication on the continent but also contributed to economic development and improved access to essential services.

Similarly, Bethlehem Tilahun Alemu, an Ethiopian entrepreneur, founded Sole Rebels, a sustainable footwear brand that combines traditional craftsmanship with eco-friendly practices. Her innovative approach to business not only garnered global recognition but also provided employment opportunities in her community while promoting sustainable practices.

These success stories underscore the transformative potential of entrepreneurship in addressing the barriers to black wealth creation. They showcase the importance of fostering an ecosystem that supports and nurtures aspiring entrepreneurs, providing them with the tools, resources, and mentorship needed to overcome challenges and realize their visions.

As Africa seeks to empower entrepreneurs and businesses, it must celebrate and learn from these success stories while also addressing the systemic barriers that persist. Encouraging innovation, providing access to finance, promoting education and skills development, and fostering an environment of collaboration are essential steps toward creating an inclusive and prosperous business landscape.

In conclusion, while systemic barriers continue to hinder black wealth creation in Africa, the success stories of African entrepreneurs serve as a beacon of hope and inspiration. By acknowledging and addressing the challenges, fostering an enabling environment, and providing targeted support, Africa can amplify the impact of entrepreneurship in driving economic growth, social change, and equitable development. Empowering African entrepreneurs is not only an economic imperative but also a pathway to dismantling the barriers that have held back the continent's full potential for far too long.

PRINCIPLE 5: SUPPORTING Entrepreneurship for Economic Empowerment

Recognizing the pivotal role of entrepreneurship in fostering economic empowerment, Chapter 6 delves into Principle 5: Supporting Entrepreneurship for Economic Empowerment. This principle underscores the critical need for concerted efforts to create an enabling environment that empowers entrepreneurs, removes obstacles, and catalyses sustainable economic growth across the African continent.

Overcoming Systemic Barriers to Black Wealth Creation

The journey of entrepreneurship is riddled with challenges, and for black entrepreneurs in Africa, these challenges are often exacerbated by systemic barriers that have historical, social, and economic roots. Systemic barriers, ranging from limited access to capital and financial resources to uneven regulatory environments, hinder the growth and sustainability of black-owned businesses.

Access to finance remains a fundamental hurdle. Black entrepreneurs often face difficulties in securing capital to start or expand their businesses due to factors such as stringent lending criteria, lack of collateral, and limited financial literacy. Financial institutions' hesitance to invest in ventures led by black entrepreneurs perpetuates cycles of inequality and hinders economic progress.

Unequal regulatory environments further impede entrepreneurship. Cumbersome bureaucratic processes, excessive licensing requirements, and inconsistent legal frameworks discourage business innovation and growth. The lack of efficient infrastructure, including reliable electricity and digital connectivity, adds additional challenges to business operations, particularly for small and medium-sized enterprises.

Moreover, historical legacies of discrimination and exclusion continue to cast long shadows. The effects of colonization, apartheid, and racial segregation have left lasting imprints on economic opportunities and social mobility. These historical injustices have led to entrenched disparities in access to education, resources, and opportunities, limiting the ability of black entrepreneurs to fully participate in economic activities.

Pathways to Overcome Barriers

Addressing systemic barriers to black wealth creation requires multifaceted approaches that promote inclusivity, level the playing field, and empower entrepreneurs. Policymakers and stakeholders must work collaboratively to develop policies and initiatives that create an enabling environment for entrepreneurs to thrive.

One essential step is to facilitate access to finance by designing innovative financial instruments, supporting microfinance initiatives, and establishing venture capital funds dedicated to supporting black entrepreneurs. Providing mentorship, business development support, and capacity-building programs can help entrepreneurs navigate challenges and build sustainable enterprises.

Simplifying regulatory processes and reducing bureaucratic hurdles can encourage entrepreneurship. Governments should prioritize streamlining business registration, licensing procedures, and tax policies to create a friendlier environment for business development. Investing in digital infrastructure and expanding access to e-commerce platforms can help overcome infrastructure challenges and unlock new markets.

Education and skills development are paramount. By investing in quality education and vocational training that equips young people with relevant skills, African nations can create a capable workforce prepared for the demands of modern entrepreneurship. Addressing historical inequalities through affirmative action and targeted policies can also contribute to leveling the playing field.

In conclusion, the journey toward empowering black entrepreneurs and dismantling systemic barriers is a complex yet essential endeavor for Africa's economic liberation. By embracing Principle 5 and implementing comprehensive strategies that address access to finance, regulatory hurdles, historical inequalities, and skills development, the continent can create an environment where entrepreneurship thrives, wealth is created, and equitable economic empowerment becomes a reality. Empowering entrepreneurs is not only an investment in individual success but a catalyst for broader economic transformation that benefits communities, nations, and the continent as a whole.

Chapter 7

Reimagining Education, Skills Development, and Gender Equality

The principle of reimagining education, skills development, and gender equality underscores the pivotal role of education in shaping Africa's economic future. In this context, examining pre-colonial education and its relevance provides valuable insights into fostering inclusive growth and sustainable development.

Pre-Colonial Education and Its Relevance

Before the advent of colonization, African societies had rich and diverse systems of education that were deeply intertwined with cultural values, practical skills, and communal learning. Education was holistic, encompassing not only academic knowledge but also social, spiritual, and vocational teachings. These indigenous educational practices played a crucial role in preparing individuals to contribute meaningfully to their communities and societies.

1. Holistic Learning: Pre-colonial education focused on a well-rounded education that cultivated various aspects of an individual's potential. It emphasized values such as responsibility, respect, and community cooperation, instilling a sense of civic duty and belonging.

2. Cultural Preservation: Education was intricately connected to the preservation of cultural heritage. Oral traditions, storytelling, and rituals were integral to the transmission of knowledge, history, and societal norms from one generation to another.

3. Vocational Skills: Practical skills were highly valued in pre-colonial education. Individuals were taught essential life skills, such as farming, craftsmanship, and trade, which not only contributed to economic self-sufficiency but also nurtured a sense of self-worth and autonomy.

4. Community Participation: Learning was a communal endeavour, involving interactions between generations and fostering a strong sense of identity and belonging within the community. Elders served as educators, passing down wisdom and experiences.

Relevance for Today's Challenges

Reimagining education based on the principles of pre-colonial learning holds significant potential for addressing contemporary challenges and advancing inclusive growth in Africa.

1. Holistic Learning for Holistic Solutions: By incorporating holistic education models, modern African societies can produce individuals who possess not only academic knowledge but also strong ethical values, critical thinking abilities, and problem-solving skills. This approach can lead to innovative solutions for complex challenges.

2. Empowering Women and Marginalized Groups: Pre-colonial education often provided opportunities for women to develop essential skills and knowledge. Reimagining education with a gender-inclusive lens can empower women to play a more significant role in economic activities and decision-making processes.

3. Cultural Identity and Innovation: Incorporating cultural elements into education can help preserve cultural heritage while fostering innovation and creativity. This integration can provide unique insights and perspectives, enabling Africa to contribute authentically to the global economy.

4. Lifelong Learning: Learning throughout one's life was a fundamental aspect of pre-colonial education. Modern education systems should emphasize lifelong learning, adaptability, and continuous skills development to keep pace with rapidly changing economic landscapes.

In reimagining education based on pre-colonial principles, Africa can build a foundation that promotes individual growth, community development, and sustainable economic progress. By recognizing the value of diverse knowledge systems, embracing gender equality, and fostering lifelong learning, Africa can overcome existing challenges and position itself for a future of inclusive and equitable prosperity.

Speculating on education without colonization's impact.

Without the influence of colonization, African education might have followed a vastly different trajectory, one that is deeply rooted in indigenous knowledge systems, cultural values, and community-driven learning. Speculating on what education could have been without colonization's impact offers a glimpse into an alternative reality where Africa's educational landscape may have thrived with a unique blend of traditional wisdom and modern knowledge.

In such a scenario, education would have been intimately connected to the land, environment, and local practices. Indigenous knowledge, passed down through generations, would have been central to the curriculum, fostering a sense of identity and pride among the youth. Learning would have been a communal effort, where elders and community members played pivotal roles in imparting skills, values, and practical wisdom.

Technical skills and vocational training would have been highly valued, aligning with the needs of the community and the local economy. These skills could range from agriculture and craftsmanship to hunting, fishing, and sustainable resource management. Apprenticeships and mentorship models might have thrived, creating a seamless transition from learning to application.

In this alternative narrative, gender equality might have flourished, with education being equally accessible to all members of society. Women's contributions and roles in various fields would have been acknowledged and celebrated, leading to a more balanced and equitable social structure. This would have not only empowered women but also contributed to a more inclusive and prosperous society.

The absence of colonization's impact on education could have resulted in a holistic approach to learning, where intellectual growth went hand in hand with ethical development. Education would have been tailored to address the specific needs of the community, fostering a sense of responsibility and interconnectedness. The accumulation of knowledge would have been guided by a deeper understanding of sustainability, leading to practices that preserve the environment and support long-term well-being.

While it's impossible to definitively determine the course of history without colonization, speculating on the potential outcomes of an education system rooted in indigenous wisdom offers a valuable perspective. It underscores the importance of reclaiming, preserving, and integrating traditional knowledge into modern education, ultimately paving the way for a more culturally rich, socially just, and economically thriving Africa.

Economic Benefits of Gender Equality

In a hypothetical scenario where gender equality had been a cornerstone of education and development in Africa, there would likely have been significant economic benefits. Gender equality goes beyond being a matter of social justice; it's also a crucial driver of economic growth and sustainable development. Here's how:

1. **Increased Workforce Participation:** When both men and women have equal access to education and employment opportunities, it results in a larger and more skilled workforce. This, in turn, boosts productivity and drives economic growth.
2. **Diverse Perspectives and Innovation:** Gender diversity in education and the workplace brings a wider range of perspectives and ideas. This diversity fosters innovation and creativity, leading to the development of new products, services, and solutions.
3. **Reduced Skills Gaps:** In many societies, women have been historically excluded from certain fields or industries. Addressing these gender-based skill gaps through inclusive education would lead to a more balanced distribution of skills across sectors, optimizing workforce potential.
4. **Entrepreneurship and Economic Resilience:** Gender-inclusive education and economic opportunities empower women to become entrepreneurs, contributing to job creation and economic resilience. Women-led businesses can also provide unique solutions to community challenges.
5. **Enhanced Human Capital:** Investing in girls' education and women's health has a positive impact on child and maternal health. Educated mothers tend to have healthier families, resulting in a stronger and more capable workforce in the long run.
6. **Decreased Income Inequality:** Gender pay gaps and unequal access to economic resources perpetuate income inequality. Promoting gender equality addresses these disparities, leading to more equitable income distribution.

7. **Sustainable Development:** Women often play a central role in natural resource management and agriculture. By involving women in sustainable development strategies, communities can better manage their resources and mitigate environmental challenges.
8. **Social Stability:** Gender inequality can contribute to social tensions and conflicts. Promoting gender equality fosters social harmony and stability, creating an environment conducive to economic development.

In summary, a scenario where gender equality was prioritized in education and development in Africa would likely have led to a more vibrant and dynamic economy. By tapping into the full potential of both men and women, societies can create a stronger foundation for sustainable growth and prosperity. Gender equality isn't just a moral imperative; it's an economic imperative that benefits everyone.

Principle 6: Equipping Citizens with Skills and Empowering Women

This principle underscores the significance of education and skill development as powerful tools for both individual empowerment and societal progress. It emphasizes the need to bridge the gender gap and ensure equal access to education and skill-building opportunities for women. By doing so, societies can tap into the full potential of their human capital, contributing to economic growth and sustainable development.

Education is not only a means of acquiring knowledge but also a catalyst for personal growth and socio-economic advancement. Before the influence of colonization, African societies possessed education systems that were closely aligned with their cultural values and needs. Reimagining education without colonization's impact involves speculating how traditional African educational models might have evolved to incorporate modern skills and knowledge while preserving cultural identity.

Moreover, gender equality is highlighted as a critical component of this principle. Empowering women with education and skills has the potential to break down barriers, challenge stereotypes, and enable them to play active roles in various spheres of society. When women are given equal opportunities, societies benefit from diverse perspectives, innovative ideas, and increased productivity.

By equipping citizens, especially women, with the skills they need to thrive in a rapidly changing world, this principle envisions a future where education is a means of fostering human potential and advancing societies. It aligns with the broader mission of "Rich but Poor" to establish a foundation of knowledge, capabilities, and equal opportunities that contribute to Africa's economic empowerment and overall well-being.

Chapter 8

Overcoming Historical Economic Legacies and Healthcare

Impact of colonization on Africa's wealth

The African continent stands as a testament to the enduring impact of historical economic imbalances and the complex interplay between its rich resources and the state of healthcare. This exploration delves into the intricate ties between historical economic legacies and the healthcare landscape, uncovering the deep-seated effects of colonization on Africa's wealth and the subsequent ramifications for its healthcare systems.

The colonization of Africa during the 19th and early 20th centuries was characterized by the aggressive exploitation of the continent's abundant resources by European powers. This era marked a period of territorial division and resource extraction, as colonial powers sought to extract valuable minerals, agricultural products, and other commodities to fuel their industrialization. The result was a systematic draining of Africa's wealth, leaving the continent economically weakened and its resources largely controlled by external entities.

These historical economic imbalances were not confined to resource extraction alone; they also gave rise to exploitative economic systems. The imposition of cash crop monocultures and other extractive economic models further entrenched Africa's role as a provider of raw materials to colonial powers. This dependence on external markets inhibited the development of local industries and hindered the growth of diverse, self-sustaining economies.

The far-reaching consequences of historical economic exploitation reverberate through Africa's healthcare systems. The underdevelopment of domestic economies directly translated into limited investments in healthcare infrastructure. This lack of investment impeded the establishment of robust healthcare systems capable of effectively addressing the health needs of African populations. Healthcare disparities became exacerbated as access to quality medical services became a luxury, particularly for marginalized communities.

Preventable diseases found fertile ground to thrive, and the lack of adequate healthcare financing perpetuated the cycle of inadequate access to essential medical services. The historical economic inequalities directly contributed to the fragmentation of healthcare delivery, leaving a large portion of the population underserved and vulnerable.

This exploration serves as a critical call to action, urging a comprehensive understanding of the persistent impact of historical economic imbalances on Africa's healthcare landscape. By dissecting the intricacies of colonization's consequences, we uncover a pressing need to break free from the shackles of the past. The journey through this exploration unveils the potential for innovative strategies, collaborative partnerships, and the resilience of African nations in forging new paths towards equitable healthcare systems that transcend the legacies of economic exploitation.

EXAMINING ECONOMIC Policies and Legacies

The current economic landscape of many African nations is intricately intertwined with the economic policies and legacies inherited from both colonial and post-colonial eras. This section delves into the complex web of economic decisions, policies, and historical circumstances that have shaped Africa's economic trajectory and continue to impact its development.

In the aftermath of colonization, newly independent African countries faced the formidable challenge of building functional economies from the fragmented economic structures left behind. Often operating within a global framework that favoured developed nations, African economies encountered obstacles that hindered their ability to compete and flourish. Trade imbalances, debt burdens, and limited access to international markets created barriers to sustainable growth.

One significant aspect of examining economic policies and legacies is understanding the role of structural adjustment programs that many African nations adopted in the latter half of the 20th century. These programs, often dictated by international financial institutions, aimed to address economic crises but frequently resulted in austerity measures, reduced public investment, and the privatization of key industries. While some argue that these measures were necessary for economic stabilization, others contend that they exacerbated inequalities and hindered long-term development.

Additionally, the legacy of economic policies is intertwined with issues of corruption and mismanagement. Some post-colonial governments struggled to establish transparent and accountable governance structures, leading to the diversion of resources and missed opportunities for economic growth. These challenges were compounded by external factors, including unfair trade practices and unfavourable terms of engagement with global markets.

Despite these challenges, there have been notable efforts by African nations to reshape economic policies and foster inclusive development. The rise of regional economic communities, such as the African Union and the East African Community, reflects a commitment to collective economic progress. These initiatives seek to harness the continent's collective potential, promote intra-African trade, and reduce reliance on external markets.

Furthermore, initiatives to promote diversification and value addition in economic sectors are gaining traction. By moving beyond the export of raw materials and embracing higher value-added industries, African countries aim to create more resilient and sustainable economies. Investment in education, technology, and entrepreneurship is crucial to driving innovation and nurturing a skilled workforce that can contribute to economic transformation.

This section highlights the nuanced relationship between economic policies, historical legacies, and the ongoing efforts to forge a more economically empowered Africa. It underscores the need for a comprehensive and context-specific approach to economic development—one that takes into account the unique challenges faced by African nations while leveraging their vast potential. Through deliberate policy choices, investment in human capital, and a commitment to equitable growth, Africa seeks to transcend historical economic constraints and chart a course toward prosperity and self-sufficiency.

Challenges in Healthcare Access and Quality

Access to quality healthcare is a fundamental human right, yet in many African countries, challenges persist in ensuring that all citizens have equitable access to essential medical services. This section examines the multifaceted issues that have contributed to inadequate healthcare access and quality, and explores the efforts being made to overcome these challenges.

Healthcare disparities across Africa are deeply rooted in historical, economic, and social factors. The legacy of colonial rule often left behind fragmented healthcare systems, where resources were disproportionately allocated to colonial administrators and settlers, while local populations were neglected. Post-independence, the task of building comprehensive and accessible healthcare infrastructure was further complicated by limited resources, economic instability, and competing developmental priorities.

One of the most critical challenges is the lack of sufficient healthcare infrastructure, including medical facilities, trained healthcare professionals, and medical supplies. Rural and remote areas often suffer the most due to insufficient clinics and hospitals, resulting in citizens having to travel long distances to access even basic medical care. Additionally, a shortage of doctors, nurses, and other medical personnel contributes to the inability to meet the healthcare needs of the population.

Another key issue is the affordability of healthcare services. Many African countries struggle with high out-of-pocket expenses for medical treatments, medications, and consultations. This can lead to people avoiding seeking medical care due to financial constraints, resulting in delayed treatment and worsened health outcomes. The absence of effective health insurance systems further compounds the challenge of ensuring affordable and accessible healthcare.

Healthcare quality is also a concern, as insufficient training, outdated medical equipment, and inadequate regulatory oversight can impact patient care. The lack of standardized healthcare protocols and guidelines can lead to variations in treatment quality and outcomes.

In some cases, preventable diseases and conditions persist due to inadequate health education and awareness programs.

Efforts to address these challenges are underway, driven by both governmental and non-governmental initiatives. Many African nations are working to strengthen their healthcare systems through increased investment in infrastructure, healthcare workforce development, and healthcare research. International partnerships and collaborations are also playing a role in improving healthcare access, with organizations providing funding, training, and technical support.

Community-based healthcare initiatives and telemedicine programs are leveraging technology to extend healthcare services to remote areas. These approaches aim to bridge geographical barriers and enhance medical consultations and diagnostics, particularly in areas with limited access to medical facilities.

The challenges in healthcare access and quality underscore the need for comprehensive and sustainable strategies to ensure that all Africans have the opportunity to lead healthy lives. Addressing historical inequities, investing in healthcare infrastructure, strengthening healthcare workforce capacity, and implementing effective health education programs are crucial steps in overcoming these challenges. By prioritizing accessible and quality healthcare, Africa can lay the foundation for a healthier and more prosperous future for its people.

Principle 7: Building Resilient Economies and Universal Healthcare

The principle of building resilient economies and ensuring universal healthcare is a critical component of Africa's journey towards sustainable development and poverty reduction. This section delves into the interconnectedness of economic stability and healthcare access, highlighting the importance of resilient economies in facilitating comprehensive and affordable healthcare for all.

Building Resilient Economies

African economies have faced various challenges, including the impact of external shocks, limited diversification, and overdependence on a narrow range of commodities. These vulnerabilities have been exacerbated by historical economic legacies, which often left nations with economic structures designed to serve colonial interests rather than indigenous development.

To build resilient economies, African nations are focusing on economic diversification, promoting innovation, and investing in critical sectors such as agriculture, manufacturing, and technology. By reducing reliance on a single industry, countries can mitigate the adverse effects of commodity price fluctuations and external shocks. Additionally, fostering an environment conducive to entrepreneurship and small business development can contribute to economic dynamism and job creation.

Investments in infrastructure, including transportation, energy, and digital connectivity, are fundamental to economic resilience. Improving connectivity both within and across countries enhances trade opportunities, facilitates access to markets, and stimulates economic growth. Moreover, infrastructure investments play a vital role in delivering essential services, including healthcare, to remote and underserved areas.

Universal Healthcare

Universal healthcare, often referred to as access to quality medical services without financial hardship, is a cornerstone of inclusive development. It embodies the idea that everyone should have access to the healthcare they need, regardless of their financial status. Achieving universal healthcare requires a combination of policies, funding mechanisms, and health system strengthening.

Healthcare financing models that pool risk and ensure broad financial protection are central to universal healthcare. Many African countries are exploring various financing strategies, including social health insurance, public funding, and community-based health schemes. These mechanisms aim to reduce out-of-pocket expenditures and enable equitable access to healthcare services.

Strengthening healthcare systems involves addressing human resource shortages, enhancing infrastructure, and implementing robust health information systems. Investments in training and retaining healthcare professionals, as well as equipping medical facilities with up-to-date technology and medical equipment, are crucial steps in ensuring that healthcare services meet quality standards.

Preventive healthcare and health education play pivotal roles in achieving universal healthcare. By promoting healthy behaviors and raising awareness about diseases, communities can reduce the burden on healthcare systems and improve overall population health. Investing in health education programs contributes to disease prevention and early detection, leading to improved health outcomes.

Inhe principle of building resilient economies and ensuring universal healthcare acknowledges the symbiotic relationship between economic development and access to quality healthcare. By diversifying economies, fostering innovation, and investing in critical sectors, African nations can create the foundation for stable and resilient economies. Simultaneously, achieving universal healthcare requires addressing financial barriers, strengthening healthcare systems, and promoting preventive healthcare measures. These efforts, when pursued hand in hand, have the potential to transform the health and well-being of African populations while contributing to sustained economic growth and prosperity.

Chapter 9

Regional Integration, Technological Advancement, and Climate Action

The intersection of regional cooperation, technological advancement, and climate action holds immense significance in Africa's pursuit of sustainable development and shared prosperity.

Importance of Regional Cooperation

Regional integration stands as a linchpin of Africa's developmental aspirations. Recognizing that collaboration across borders can yield greater benefits than isolated efforts, African nations are coming together to address common challenges and harness collective opportunities.

Initiatives like the African Continental Free Trade Area (AfCFTA) exemplify the commitment to economic integration. AfCFTA aims to establish a unified market across the continent, fostering trade and investment among African nations. This approach fosters economic diversification, job creation, and overall growth.

Beyond economic gains, regional collaboration extends to security enhancement, infrastructure development, and knowledge exchange. Joint initiatives promote infrastructure connectivity and cooperation, crucial for stimulating trade and bolstering social and economic advancement.

Technological Advancement as Catalyst

Technological innovation is a cornerstone of Africa's transformation. Embracing innovative technologies can fast-track progress across sectors like agriculture, health, education, and finance. Access to digital platforms, mobile technologies, and internet connectivity empowers citizens and businesses, bridging information gaps and enhancing service delivery.

Innovations such as mobile banking and digital payment systems have extended financial inclusivity, particularly in regions with limited banking infrastructure. E-commerce platforms enable entrepreneurs to reach wider markets, propelling economic growth and job opportunities.

Technology plays a pivotal role in addressing healthcare disparities. Telemedicine, remote diagnostics, and mobile health applications expand medical services to remote areas, improving access to healthcare and reducing disparities.

Commitment to Climate Action

Africa's vulnerability to climate change necessitates robust climate action to ensure sustainable development. Climate impacts, from droughts to floods, affect livelihoods, food security, and economic stability. Effective mitigation requires collective efforts to reduce emissions and bolster climate resilience.

African countries are investing in renewable energy sources such as solar, wind, and hydroelectric power. These efforts reduce carbon emissions, enhance energy security, and promote sustainable development.

Integrating climate considerations into development planning enhances resilience to climate risks. Strategies like sustainable land management and climate-smart agriculture contribute to ecosystem preservation and food security.

The interplay between regional integration, technological advancement, and climate action is pivotal to Africa's sustainable development. By fostering regional collaboration, embracing technological breakthroughs, and prioritizing climate-resilient strategies, Africa can navigate complexities and harness opportunities for inclusive growth. This holistic approach will empower Africa to unlock its economic potential while safeguarding its environment for generations to come.

Addressing Challenges for Collective Growth

The importance of regional cooperation and technological advancement in Africa cannot be overstated, particularly in the face of shared challenges that transcend national borders. Through collaborative efforts, African nations can collectively address these challenges and drive sustainable growth.

Infrastructure Development and Connectivity

One of the critical challenges facing Africa is the need for robust and interconnected infrastructure. Regional integration enables the pooling of resources and expertise to build vital infrastructure such as roads, railways, ports, and energy networks. These interconnected systems facilitate trade, boost economic activity, and enhance regional stability.

Infrastructure projects also extend to digital connectivity. Expanding access to reliable internet services bridges the digital divide, ensuring that all citizens can participate in the digital economy and access critical information and services.

Conflict Resolution and Peacebuilding

Internal conflicts and political instability have hindered Africa's progress for decades. Regional cooperation serves as a platform for conflict resolution and peacebuilding. By engaging in diplomatic efforts and collaborative strategies, neighboring nations can help mitigate conflicts and promote stability.

African institutions like the African Union (AU) play a pivotal role in mediating disputes and preventing conflicts from escalating. By fostering unity and cooperation among member states, the AU contributes to a more peaceful and stable continent.

Leveraging Technological Leapfrogging

Technological advancement offers Africa the opportunity to leapfrog certain developmental stages, accelerating progress. Traditional barriers, such as limited access to physical infrastructure, can be bypassed through innovative technologies.

Mobile technology, for instance, has transformed financial services. Mobile banking and payment platforms provide access to financial tools that were previously unavailable to large segments of the population. This leapfrogging effect empowers individuals economically, even in remote areas.

Similarly, advancements in renewable energy technologies allow Africa to reduce its reliance on fossil fuels and transition to cleaner energy sources. The continent's abundance of solar energy, for instance, can be harnessed to improve energy access and reduce carbon emissions.

Adopting Climate-Resilient Practices

Africa is disproportionately affected by climate change, but concerted efforts at the regional level can enhance resilience. Collaborative strategies to manage water resources, conserve ecosystems, and implement sustainable agriculture practices are crucial.

Through sharing knowledge, expertise, and best practices, African countries can collectively develop climate adaptation strategies. This includes early warning systems for natural disasters, climate-responsive agriculture, and sustainable land and water management.

The importance of regional integration, technological advancement, and climate action in Africa is evident in their potential to address shared challenges and accelerate progress. By collaborating across borders, leveraging innovative technologies, and prioritizing climate resilience, African nations can collectively pave the way for a more prosperous and sustainable future.

Harnessing Renewable Energy Potential

Africa possesses an abundance of renewable energy resources, including solar, wind, hydro, and geothermal power. Harnessing these resources has the potential to not only address the continent's energy deficit but also drive sustainable development and mitigate climate change.

Solar Energy: A Vast Resource

Solar energy is one of the most promising renewable resources in Africa. With its abundant sunlight, the continent has the potential to generate a significant portion of its energy needs from solar power. Solar photovoltaic systems can be deployed on rooftops, in rural communities, and in large-scale solar farms.

Off-grid solar solutions, such as solar lanterns and home solar systems, have already transformed energy access for millions of Africans. These solutions provide clean and affordable energy to remote and underserved areas, improving lighting, powering small appliances, and supporting economic activities.

Wind Power: Tapping into Wind Resources

Wind energy also holds great promise for Africa's energy future. Many regions across the continent experience consistent and strong winds that can be harnessed for power generation. Wind farms can be established both onshore and offshore, contributing to national and regional energy grids.

Wind energy projects can provide not only electricity but also employment opportunities and local economic growth. By investing in wind power, African countries can diversify their energy mix and reduce their dependence on fossil fuels.

Hydroelectric Power: Utilizing Water Resources

Africa's numerous rivers and water bodies offer significant potential for hydroelectric power generation. Large-scale hydroelectric dams can provide consistent and reliable energy, supporting industrialization and urbanization. However, such projects also need to be carefully planned to minimize environmental and social impacts.

Small-scale hydroelectric projects can also play a crucial role in decentralized energy generation. These projects can provide electricity to rural communities, powering homes, schools, and health clinics.

Geothermal Energy: Tapping Earth's Heat

Geothermal energy harnesses the natural heat stored within the Earth's crust. Africa's East African Rift System provides ample geothermal resources that can be tapped for power generation. Geothermal power plants are environmentally friendly, emitting minimal greenhouse gases and requiring relatively small land areas.

Investing in geothermal energy can contribute to energy security, reduce greenhouse gas emissions, and stimulate local economic development. Moreover, geothermal resources can provide baseload power, complementing intermittent renewable sources like solar and wind.

Advancing Renewable Energy Technologies

While Africa's renewable energy potential is undeniable, realizing this potential requires technological advancements, supportive policies, and investment. Collaborative efforts at the regional level can facilitate the transfer of expertise and resources among African nations.

harnessing Africa's renewable energy potential holds the key to achieving sustainable energy access, driving economic growth, and mitigating climate change. By strategically developing solar, wind, hydro, and geothermal resources, African countries can make significant strides towards a more sustainable and prosperous future.

Principle 8: Fostering Regional Integration, Technology, and Sustainability

African nations are realizing the power of collaboration and regional integration as a means to accelerate development, harness technological advancements, and address pressing sustainability challenges. Principle 8 underscores the importance of fostering unity among African countries, leveraging technology, and adopting sustainable practices to pave the way for a brighter future.

Collaboration for Collective Growth

Regional integration involves forging closer ties and cooperation among African nations to promote economic growth, trade, and social development. Organizations like the African Union (AU) and regional economic communities (RECs) are working to create platforms for collaboration, aiming to unlock the full potential of Africa's combined resources and markets.

Through regional integration, African countries can pool resources, share knowledge, and jointly address shared challenges, such as infrastructure development, cross-border trade barriers, and security concerns. This collective approach can amplify the impact of development initiatives and create a more favorable environment for attracting investment and fostering innovation.

Leveraging Technology for Progress

Technology has the potential to be a powerful catalyst for development across various sectors in Africa. Rapid advancements in information and communication technology (ICT), digitalization, and artificial intelligence (AI) are reshaping economies and societies. African nations can harness technology to leapfrog traditional development paths and unlock new opportunities.

Mobile technology, for instance, has already transformed financial services through mobile banking and digital payment systems. E-commerce platforms are connecting small businesses with a broader customer base. Digital solutions are enhancing healthcare access and delivery, and e-learning platforms are revolutionizing education.

Investing in technology infrastructure, fostering digital literacy, and encouraging innovation ecosystems are critical steps towards realizing the potential of technology for sustainable development.

Sustainability for Future Generations

Sustainability is at the heart of Africa's journey towards prosperity. Balancing economic development with environmental conservation and social equity is vital for long-term growth. African nations are increasingly recognizing the importance of adopting sustainable practices across sectors such as agriculture, energy, and urban planning.

Promoting sustainable practices, such as agro-ecological farming methods, renewable energy adoption, and green urban planning, can lead to improved resource management, reduced environmental degradation, and enhanced resilience against climate change impacts.

By adhering to sustainable principles, African countries can ensure that development is not at the expense of future generations. This approach aligns with the global commitment to achieving the United Nations Sustainable Development Goals (SDGs) and contributes to the overall well-being of African societies.

This pprinciple emphasizes the value of regional collaboration, technology adoption, and sustainability as drivers of Africa's development. By working together, harnessing technological advancements, and embracing sustainable practices, African nations can collectively shape a more prosperous, equitable, and sustainable future for the continent and its people.

Chapter 10

Enhancing Agricultural Productivity, Water Access, and Youth Empowerment

Modernizing Agricultural Practices and Value Chains

The agricultural sector has always been a cornerstone of Africa's economy and livelihoods. Within the context of Principle 9, the focus is on modernizing agricultural practices and value chains to foster sustainable growth, ensure food security, and empower communities.

Innovative Approaches to Farming

Modernizing agriculture entails embracing innovative techniques and technologies that can amplify productivity while minimizing negative environmental impacts. Techniques like precision agriculture, which utilizes satellite data and advanced analytics, enable farmers to optimize resource allocation, reduce waste, and enhance crop yields.

Value Chain Enhancement

Modernizing agriculture goes beyond the fields; it extends to the entire value chain, from production to distribution. Developing efficient post-harvest handling, storage, and transportation systems can significantly reduce losses and ensure that produce reaches markets in optimal condition. Value chain enhancements also encompass processing raw agricultural products into value-added goods, contributing to economic diversification and increased income for farmers.

Empowering Smallholder Farmers

Smallholder farmers play a crucial role in African agriculture. Empowering them with knowledge, skills, and access to resources can uplift their productivity and living standards. Training in modern farming practices, sustainable land management, and access to credit can help smallholders transition from subsistence farming to profitable enterprises.

Youth Engagement

Engaging the youth in agriculture is imperative for sustainable development. The sector presents opportunities for entrepreneurship, innovation, and technology adoption. By promoting agriculture as a viable and attractive career option, youth can become agents of change in driving modernization, increasing productivity, and transforming rural communities.

Water Management

Efficient water management is central to agricultural sustainability. Adopting water-saving technologies, such as drip irrigation and rainwater harvesting, can help conserve this precious resource. Ensuring equitable access to water for agricultural purposes is essential for supporting livelihoods and preventing conflicts over water resources.

In essence, modernizing agricultural practices and value chains forms a cornerstone of Africa's journey toward equitable economic development. It not only boosts productivity but also ensures food security, empowers smallholder farmers, engages the youth, and contributes to environmental sustainability. By embracing innovation and focusing on a holistic approach to agriculture, African nations can pave the way for a brighter and more prosperous future.

Addressing Water Scarcity and Sanitation

Water scarcity is a critical challenge across many parts of Africa, impacting both agricultural productivity and human well-being. Within the context of Principle 9, addressing water scarcity and improving sanitation is paramount for sustainable development.

Water Scarcity: Implications for Agriculture

Agriculture is a water-intensive sector, and water scarcity can have profound effects on crop yields and livestock. Efficient water management practices, coupled with drought-resistant crop varieties, can help mitigate the impact of water scarcity on agricultural productivity. Additionally, the recycling and reuse of water for irrigation can stretch available resources.

Improving Sanitation and Health

Access to clean and safe water is closely linked to improved sanitation and health outcomes. Lack of proper sanitation facilities can lead to the spread of waterborne diseases, impacting communities' well-being and reducing their productivity. Investments in sanitation infrastructure, along with awareness campaigns on proper hygiene practices, can contribute to better health and increased productivity.

Integrated Water Resource Management

Effective water resource management requires an integrated approach that considers the needs of agriculture, industry, and communities. This involves developing policies and strategies that balance water allocation for various uses while ensuring the sustainability of water sources. Integrated water resource management also involves engaging local communities and stakeholders in decision-making processes.

Climate Resilience

Climate change poses additional challenges to water availability and agricultural productivity. As weather patterns become more unpredictable, implementing climate-resilient agricultural practices becomes essential. Techniques such as agroforestry, soil conservation, and rainwater harvesting can help mitigate the effects of climate change on water resources and agricultural production.

Empowering Youth in Agriculture

Engaging youth in agriculture is a multifaceted approach that involves education, skills development, and access to resources. Youth-led initiatives can be instrumental in addressing water scarcity by promoting water-efficient farming techniques and advocating for sustainable water management practices. Empowering youth as agents of change in water and sanitation efforts can contribute to more inclusive and resilient communities.

Addressing water scarcity and sanitation challenges is a pivotal step towards enhancing agricultural productivity and empowering youth. By embracing innovative water management strategies, promoting climate-resilient practices, and fostering youth engagement, African nations can build a more sustainable and prosperous future. Through Principle 9, the journey towards agro-industrialization, water management, and youth development gains momentum, steering Africa closer to economic empowerment and equitable growth.

Fostering youth entrepreneurship and employment

Empowering the youth is pivotal for Africa's economic transformation. Unemployment among young people remains a pressing concern, stifling growth and potential. Efforts to enhance agricultural productivity must include strategies to engage and empower the youth. By equipping them with modern farming techniques, business skills, and access to resources, they can become the driving force behind innovative agricultural practices.

Encouraging entrepreneurship among the youth within the agricultural sector can revitalize rural economies and alleviate urban migration. Training programs, mentorship initiatives, and access to micro-financing can help aspiring young farmers overcome challenges and establish successful agribusinesses. Youth-led agricultural ventures can not only contribute to increased productivity but also inspire innovation across the entire value chain.

The principle of equipping citizens with skills, as well as fostering youth development, is essential in this context. Young Africans need access to quality education that aligns with the demands of modern agriculture. This education should encompass traditional knowledge alongside cutting-edge technologies, ensuring that the youth are prepared to leverage advancements for the continent's agricultural renaissance.

Empowering the youth within the realm of agricultural productivity and water access is more than just an economic strategy – it's a means to cultivate a new generation of leaders, innovators, and change-makers. By addressing the challenges youth face in agriculture and providing them with the necessary tools and opportunities, Africa can unlock the immense potential that lies within its young population. This empowerment contributes not only to sustainable farming practices but also to broader socio-economic growth and the realization of a prosperous continent.

Principle 9: Agro-industrialization, Water Management, and Youth Development

The principle of Agro-industrialization encapsulates a transformative vision for Africa's agricultural sector. It involves moving beyond subsistence farming and traditional methods to embrace modern, technology-driven approaches. Agro-industrialization envisions a shift from simply cultivating crops to creating value-added products, processing raw materials, and establishing an interconnected agricultural value chain. This transformation holds the potential to elevate Africa's status from being solely a source of raw materials to becoming a hub of agricultural innovation and production.

Agro-industrialization presents multifaceted benefits. By diversifying agricultural activities, such as food processing, agribusinesses can generate higher income streams and enhance employment opportunities. The youth, in particular, can harness these opportunities to channel their creativity into developing new products, improving efficiency, and driving growth.

Efficient water management stands at the core of sustainable agricultural development. As climate change poses increasing challenges to water availability, adopting innovative water-saving techniques becomes imperative. Modern irrigation methods, rainwater harvesting, and improved water infrastructure can mitigate the risks posed by changing weather patterns. Ensuring equitable water access for smallholder farmers, who constitute a significant portion of Africa's agricultural workforce, is essential for their livelihoods and productivity.

The intertwined nature of these principles highlights the holistic approach needed for successful youth development in agriculture. Agro-industrialization can create an environment conducive to youth-driven entrepreneurship, providing them with opportunities to innovate within the entire value chain. Meanwhile, proper water management safeguards against potential disruptions to these activities, securing the livelihoods of both established and aspiring farmers.

Youth development, particularly in the context of Agro-industrialization and water management, aligns with the broader agenda of sustainable development in Africa. By focusing on equipping young people with the skills and resources they need to excel in these sectors, Africa can harness their potential as agents of change. Engaging the youth in these transformative processes contributes not only to agricultural growth but also to the realization of a more prosperous and resilient continent.

Chapter 11

Cultural Heritage, Quality Healthcare, and Urbanization

Africa's cultural heritage is a treasure trove that holds immense economic potential. The richness and diversity of African cultures, traditions, and arts can serve as powerful drivers of economic growth. Cultural tourism, in particular, presents an avenue for showcasing this heritage to the world while simultaneously generating revenue for local communities. By preserving and promoting cultural landmarks, traditional crafts, and indigenous practices, Africa can tap into the global tourism industry, creating sustainable livelihoods and contributing to the continent's economic prosperity.

Economic Potential of Africa's Cultural Heritage

Africa's rich cultural heritage holds immense economic potential that remains largely untapped. The continent's diverse history, traditions, languages, and artistic expressions create a unique tapestry that can be leveraged for economic growth. Cultural tourism, which involves visitors exploring and experiencing local cultures, traditions, and heritage sites, presents a promising avenue for revenue generation.

The demand for authentic cultural experiences is on the rise globally, and Africa possesses a wealth of cultural assets that can attract both domestic and international tourists. Traditional music, dance, art, literature, festivals, and historical landmarks offer a glimpse into Africa's vibrant past and present. By promoting cultural tourism, African nations can not only generate income but also create job opportunities in various sectors such as hospitality, transportation, and handicraft production.

Investing in the preservation and promotion of cultural heritage also contributes to identity formation and community pride. Local artisans, performers, and cultural practitioners can benefit from increased visibility and market access. Additionally, the revenue generated from cultural tourism can be reinvested in local communities to improve infrastructure, education, and healthcare.

Recognizing the economic value of cultural heritage aligns with the principle of sustainable urbanization, as it encourages the development of cultural tourism hubs and creative districts within cities. However, it's important to approach cultural tourism with sensitivity, ensuring that communities are active participants in the process and that cultural practices are preserved and respected. By unlocking the economic potential of Africa's cultural heritage, nations can simultaneously promote economic growth, preserve their heritage, and enrich the overall cultural landscape.

Investing in Healthcare and Education

Central to Africa's journey towards prosperity is the strategic investment in quality healthcare and education. These pillars are not only fundamental human rights but also crucial drivers of economic growth and development. By prioritizing healthcare and education, African nations can empower their citizens with the tools and resources needed to thrive in an increasingly interconnected world.

1. **Healthcare Transformation:** Adequate healthcare is essential for a productive workforce and a healthy population. Investing in healthcare infrastructure, training healthcare professionals, and ensuring access to essential services can lead to improved health outcomes. Addressing health challenges such as infectious diseases, maternal and child mortality, and non-communicable diseases is crucial for building a strong and resilient society.
2. **Educational Advancement:** Quality education equips individuals with the skills and knowledge needed to participate in the modern economy. Preparing students for the challenges of the future requires curricula that integrate critical thinking, problem-solving, and digital literacy. Moreover, investing in teacher training and educational technology can enhance the learning experience and empower the next generation to drive innovation and change.
3. **Empowerment of Women:** Gender equality is closely linked to both healthcare and education. When women have equal access to education and healthcare, societies benefit from their contributions to the workforce, governance, and community development. Empowering women also leads to improved family planning, maternal and child health, and overall social well-being.

Investing in healthcare and education aligns with the principle of equipping citizens with skills and empowering women. By ensuring access to quality healthcare services and education opportunities, African nations can create an environment where individuals are healthy, educated, and capable of participating meaningfully in their communities and economies. This holistic approach fosters a cycle of development, where healthy and educated individuals contribute to the growth and prosperity of their nations.

Managing Urbanization and Promoting Smart Cities

The rapid pace of urbanization in Africa presents both opportunities and challenges for sustainable development. As cities continue to grow, effective urban planning and the promotion of smart cities become imperative to ensure that urban areas are livable, efficient, and environmentally sustainable.

1. **Harnessing Urban Potential:** Urbanization can serve as a catalyst for economic growth and innovation. Cities are hubs of economic activity, cultural exchange, and technological advancement. By concentrating resources, infrastructure, and human capital, cities create the conditions for businesses to thrive, jobs to be generated, and ideas to flourish.
2. **Sustainable Infrastructure:** As urban populations increase, the demand for infrastructure intensifies. Developing efficient and sustainable transportation systems, energy sources, and waste management solutions are essential to prevent congestion, pollution, and resource depletion. Smart city technologies, such as renewable energy integration and digital connectivity, can enhance urban living standards while reducing environmental impacts.
3. **Preserving Cultural Identity:** Urbanization poses the challenge of preserving cultural heritage and identity amidst

rapid change. African cities have a rich cultural tapestry that can be leveraged for economic development through cultural tourism and creative industries. Balancing modernization with the preservation of cultural landmarks, traditions, and values is critical to maintaining a sense of identity and belonging.

4. **Inclusive Urban Development:** Ensuring that the benefits of urbanization are equitably distributed is a cornerstone of sustainable urban development. Addressing issues of inequality, housing affordability, and access to basic services is crucial for fostering social cohesion and preventing urban disparities from becoming barriers to progress.

The principle of cultural tourism, human capital, and sustainable urbanization aligns with the imperative of managing urbanization and promoting smart cities. By adopting comprehensive urban planning strategies that prioritize environmental sustainability, social inclusion, and cultural preservation, African nations can create cities that are not only economically vibrant but also conducive to the well-being and prosperity of their residents.

PRINCIPLE 10: CULTURAL Tourism, Human Capital, and Sustainable Urbanization

Promoting Sustainable Urbanization Through Cultural Tourism

Africa's cultural heritage is a treasure trove of traditions, stories, art, and practices that have been passed down through generations. Recognizing the economic potential of cultural tourism, African nations are harnessing their rich cultural diversity to attract visitors and generate revenue.

1. **Cultural Tourism as an Economic Driver:** Cultural tourism involves showcasing the unique cultural aspects of a region to visitors. This can include heritage sites, festivals, traditional craftsmanship, and indigenous practices. By investing in cultural tourism, African nations can create jobs, stimulate local economies, and diversify revenue streams beyond traditional industries.
2. **Preserving Cultural Identity:** Cultural tourism not only brings economic benefits but also contributes to the preservation of cultural heritage. When communities see the value of their traditions and customs, they are more likely to actively protect and pass them on to future generations. This helps prevent the erosion of cultural identity in the face of globalization.
3. **Fostering Cross-Cultural Understanding:** Cultural tourism fosters intercultural exchange, breaking down stereotypes and promoting understanding between visitors and local communities. It can also empower communities to tell their own stories and challenge misconceptions about Africa, contributing to a more accurate and nuanced global perception of the continent.
4. **Sustainable Practices:** To ensure the long-term viability of cultural tourism, sustainable practices are essential. This includes responsible tourism management that minimizes negative environmental impacts, respects local cultures, and involves communities in decision-making processes.

Investing in Human Capital: Education and Health for All

For Africa to truly thrive, it must invest in its greatest resource: its people. Education and healthcare are pivotal in shaping human capital, empowering individuals with the knowledge and well-being necessary for meaningful contributions to society.

1. **Quality Education:** Quality education equips individuals with the skills, knowledge, and critical thinking abilities needed for personal growth and socio-economic advancement. By focusing on relevant curricula, skilled teachers, and inclusive policies, African nations can empower their citizens to become active participants in their own development.
2. **Gender Equality:** Ensuring equal access to education and healthcare for all genders is not only a matter of human rights but also smart economics. Empowering women with education and healthcare opportunities enhances their socio-economic contributions, improves family well-being, and drives overall national development.
3. **Universal Healthcare:** Access to quality healthcare is a fundamental right that underpins individual productivity and overall societal health. Establishing robust healthcare systems that provide preventive, curative, and rehabilitative services ensures that citizens are healthy and able to contribute to their communities.
4. **Healthy and Skilled Workforce:** A population that is educated and healthy becomes the backbone of a nation's workforce. With proper education and healthcare, individuals can pursue diverse career paths, engage in innovation, and drive economic growth.

Chapter 12

Public-Private Partnerships, Innovation, and Governance

Collaborative Approaches to Development

In the intricate tapestry of Africa's economic advancement, collaborative approaches to development have emerged as a vital thread interweaving the public and private sectors. This segment delves into the dynamic world of public-private partnerships (PPPs), innovation ecosystems, and the pivotal role of governance in steering the continent towards sustainable growth. It serves as a call to recognize the transformative power of collaboration, technological innovation, and transparent governance in shaping Africa's trajectory of progress.

Public-Private Partnerships (PPPs): Bridging Visions

At the core of effective development lies collaboration, the force that bridges the aspirations of governments, businesses, civil society, and local communities. Public-private partnerships embody this harmonious synergy, creating a platform where resources, expertise, and collective ambitions converge to address complex challenges. Across the African continent, we observe a range of PPP models unfurling, catalyzing sectors such as infrastructure, healthcare, education, and more.

PPPs epitomize the ethos of shared responsibility, blending the strengths of both sectors to catalyze sustainable outcomes. These alliances infuse capital and innovation into sectors demanding transformative change. Once-daunting infrastructure projects are now realized with renewed vigor as public and private sectors collaborate to enhance connectivity, elevate livelihoods, and propel economic expansion. The narrative of PPPs speaks to strategic alignments, transcending conventional barriers and generating holistic, inclusive development. However, their effectiveness hinges upon robust governance structures, mechanisms of accountability, and a well-defined allocation of roles and responsibilities.

Innovation Ecosystems: Forging the Future

While collaboration is the cornerstone, innovation is the keystone, infusing vitality into the development landscape. Innovation ecosystems, nurtured through partnerships, lay the foundation for sustainable growth. In the interconnected world of the 21st century, technological advancement is a linchpin for progress. African nations, recognizing this reality, are fostering innovation hubs, accelerators, and incubators to nurture local talents, catalyze entrepreneurial vigor, and spur technological transformation.

These ecosystems offer fertile ground for creativity and experimentation, channeling the energy of young minds into tangible solutions. They energize startups, providing mentorship, networks, and funding avenues that transform abstract ideas into concrete products and services. The symbiotic relationship between the public and private sectors creates an environment conducive to innovation, where governments provide enabling policies, infrastructural support, and research institutions collaborate to drive knowledge creation. This alliance testifies to the mutual benefits that collaboration and innovation bring, forging a path to self-sufficiency, economic resilience, and global competitiveness.

Governance: Navigating the Nexus

In the intricate mosaic of public-private partnerships and innovation, the role of governance stands as a linchpin. Effective governance sets the course, ensuring that collaborations remain accountable, transparent, and aligned with broader societal goals. The interplay of state institutions, regulatory frameworks, and legal mechanisms forms the foundation for equitable partnerships. It safeguards against risks, enhances investor confidence, and mitigates imbalances that can arise from vague governance structures.

Transparent governance fosters an enabling environment for innovation, curbing the risk of monopoly and promoting healthy competition. It paves the way for fair play, safeguarding intellectual property rights, and incentivizing entrepreneurs to harness their creative potential. Equally crucial is the principle of democratic governance, where the voice of all stakeholders is heard, and inclusivity prevails. When governance embraces these principles, public-private partnerships flourish, and innovation ecosystems thrive, collectively propelling Africa towards a future of shared prosperity and self-determined growth.

In the unfolding narrative of public-private partnerships, innovation, and governance, this segment underscores the power of collaboration, innovation, and transparent governance in shaping Africa's development trajectory. It resonates with the overarching vision of the book, "Rich but Poor," by outlining a comprehensive blueprint that positions Africa at the forefront of global progress through partnerships, ingenuity, and principled governance.

Fostering Innovation Ecosystems: Cultivating Africa's Creative Potential

In the pursuit of sustainable development and prosperity, fostering innovation ecosystems stands as a strategic imperative for Africa. These ecosystems provide fertile ground where ideas germinate, creativity blossoms, and transformative solutions take root. By nurturing innovation ecosystems, Africa can tap into its immense creative reservoir to address its unique challenges and pave the way for a brighter future.

Creating Collaborative Spaces for Innovation

At the core of innovation ecosystems are collaborative spaces that serve as incubators for creativity and invention. These spaces can be physical, such as innovation hubs, co-working centers, and research institutes, or virtual platforms that connect minds across vast distances. What unites these spaces is their capacity to cultivate an environment where diverse individuals converge, exchange ideas, and collaborate on projects that have the potential to reshape industries and societies.

Nurturing a Culture of Experimentation

Innovation ecosystems are catalysts for nurturing a culture of experimentation and risk-taking. They encourage individuals to challenge conventions, think beyond boundaries, and translate abstract concepts into tangible realities. By offering access to mentorship, funding opportunities, and cutting-edge facilities, these ecosystems empower innovators to test, refine, and iterate their ideas. This iterative process of trial and error cultivates breakthrough innovations that can lead to profound change.

Catalyzing Local Problem-Solving

An essential attribute of innovation ecosystems is their capacity to tackle local challenges with globally relevant solutions. From devising innovative healthcare solutions tailored to specific African contexts to advancing sustainable agricultural practices that combat food insecurity, these ecosystems serve as crucibles for problem-solving. By bringing together experts from various fields, innovation ecosystems facilitate interdisciplinary collaborations that yield holistic solutions to complex issues.

Driving Economic Growth and Entrepreneurship

Innovation ecosystems are not only engines of innovation but also drivers of economic growth and entrepreneurship. By nurturing these ecosystems, Africa can stimulate a wave of entrepreneurship that generates job opportunities and cultivates economic resilience. Start-ups, small and medium-sized enterprises (SMEs), and established companies can benefit from the resources, networks, and support networks that these ecosystems offer. This dynamic environment fosters the creation of diverse economies and contributes to reducing vulnerability to external economic shocks.

Convergence with Principle 11: Collaborative Governance

The endeavor to foster innovation ecosystems aligns harmoniously with the principles of collaborative governance, as highlighted in Principle 11. Partnerships between governments, private enterprises, educational institutions, and civil society organizations are pivotal for supplying the essential resources and expertise needed to nurture innovation ecosystems. Research-driven policies grounded in local realities guide the formulation of innovation strategies. The democratic governance framework ensures equitable distribution of the benefits from these ecosystems, while giving citizens a voice in shaping their trajectory.

Empowering Africa's Creative Potential

Fostering innovation ecosystems signifies a pivotal step toward harnessing Africa's creative potential for sustainable development. By providing the infrastructure, resources, and nurturing environment for innovation, Africa can shift its role from a technology consumer to a technology creator. This transition not only positions Africa to effectively address its pressing challenges but also empowers it to play a leading role on the global stage in innovation, entrepreneurship, and transformative change.

Ensuring Fair Legal Systems and Governance: Building the Foundation for Equitable Development

In the pursuit of inclusive and sustainable development, the role of fair legal systems and effective governance cannot be overstated. These pillars lay the foundation for equitable progress by fostering an environment where rights are protected, justice is upheld, and opportunities are accessible to all. By ensuring that legal frameworks are just and governance is transparent, Africa can pave the way for holistic growth that benefits every citizen.

Upholding Rule of Law and Protecting Rights

Fair legal systems are characterized by the rule of law, which ensures that laws are applied impartially and that individuals are treated equitably. The establishment of a robust judicial system that upholds human rights, property rights, and contractual obligations is essential. When citizens can trust in the impartiality and predictability of legal processes, they are more likely to engage in economic activities, invest in their communities, and contribute to the overall development of society.

Transparency and Accountability in Governance

Effective governance hinges on transparency, accountability, and the active participation of citizens in decision-making processes. Transparent governance fosters trust between governments and their constituents, leading to better allocation of resources, reduced corruption, and increased public participation. By embracing open data, citizen engagement platforms, and mechanisms for holding leaders accountable, Africa can ensure that public resources are used efficiently and equitably.

Combatting Corruption and Ensuring Justice

Corruption undermines development by diverting resources away from essential services and eroding trust in public institutions. Fair legal systems are instrumental in combating corruption, as they ensure that those who engage in corrupt practices are held accountable. Independent anti-corruption agencies, whistleblower protections, and stringent penalties for corrupt activities are crucial components of this endeavor. When individuals have confidence in the fairness and efficacy of legal mechanisms, they are more likely to report corruption and contribute to a culture of integrity.

Inclusivity and Protection of Vulnerable Populations

Fair legal systems and governance prioritize the protection of vulnerable populations, including women, children, marginalized communities, and minorities. Legal frameworks that address discrimination, violence, and social injustices are essential for creating an inclusive society. Additionally, effective governance mechanisms ensure that policies and programs are designed to uplift those who are most in need, reducing disparities and promoting social cohesion.

The focus on ensuring fair legal systems and governance aligns seamlessly with Principle 11, which highlights the significance of partnerships, research, and democratic governance. Collaborative partnerships between governments, civil society organizations, and international institutions can provide the resources and expertise needed to strengthen legal systems and promote good governance practices. Evidence-based research informs the design of legal reforms and policies, ensuring that they are effective and tailored to local contexts. Finally, democratic governance empowers citizens to actively participate in shaping the legal and governance frameworks that impact their lives.

Paving the Way for Equitable Development

Fair legal systems and effective governance are the cornerstones upon which equitable development is built. By upholding the rule of law, promoting transparency, and ensuring justice for all, Africa can create an environment where individuals have the confidence to invest, innovate, and contribute to the growth of their communities. Moreover, inclusive governance that protects the rights of all citizens fosters social harmony and resilience, setting the stage for sustainable progress that leaves no one behind.

Principle 11: Partnerships, Research, and Democratic Governance

In the journey towards Africa's economic transformation, the principle of fostering partnerships, conducting research, and embracing democratic governance emerges as a cornerstone for sustainable progress. This principle underscores the importance of collaboration, evidence-based decision-making, and accountable governance in shaping Africa's trajectory towards prosperity.

Collaborative Approaches for Holistic Development

The notion of partnerships transcends traditional boundaries and emphasizes the need for collective action. Public-private partnerships (PPPs) stand as a key instrument in this endeavor, where governments, businesses, and civil society converge to address complex challenges. By combining resources, expertise, and perspectives, PPPs unlock innovative solutions that may otherwise remain inaccessible. These collaborations extend to regional and international dimensions, leveraging shared goals and pooling resources to tackle continental issues.

Unleashing the Power of Research

Research acts as a guiding compass, illuminating the path forward through informed decision-making. In the African context, research tailored to the continent's unique challenges is pivotal. It provides the empirical foundation for policy formulation, identifies opportunities, and assesses the efficacy of interventions. Research institutions, both domestic and international, play a pivotal role in generating knowledge that shapes policies and practices. Investment in research capacity and infrastructure empowers African experts to contribute to global dialogues while addressing local priorities.

Democratic Governance for Accountable Development

Democratic governance, underpinned by transparent institutions and citizen participation, forms the bedrock of sustainable development. Strong democratic systems enhance accountability, foster inclusive policies, and mitigate corruption. Engaged citizens become partners in decision-making, ensuring that policies align with the needs and aspirations of the people. Democratic governance extends beyond the political realm, encompassing economic and social spheres. It lays the foundation for just and equitable development that leaves no one behind.

Amplifying African Voices through Research and Advocacy

Research isn't confined to data collection; it's a catalyst for change. Through evidence-based research, advocacy efforts gain credibility and momentum. Civil society organizations, think tanks, and academic institutions play a crucial role in amplifying the voices of marginalized communities, advocating for policy changes, and holding governments and corporations accountable. These efforts foster a culture of responsiveness and adaptability, driving development strategies that are attuned to real-world challenges.

In summary, Principle 11 underscores the importance of collaborative partnerships, research-driven decision-making, and democratic governance as essential pillars for Africa's transformation. By embracing partnerships that transcend boundaries, leveraging research for informed choices, and upholding democratic values, African nations can pave a sustainable path towards inclusive prosperity. This principle resonates as a call to action, reminding us that Africa's future is shaped not by isolated efforts, but by collective commitment to progress.

Conclusion

Summarizing key findings and encouraging collective efforts.

Vision for Africa's economic future.

As we journey through the chapters of "Rich but Poor," the intricate tapestry of Africa's story unfolds, revealing a landscape rich in natural resources yet marked by persistent poverty. This exploration has delved into the heart of Africa's challenges, weaving together historical complexities, social dynamics, and economic intricacies to present a comprehensive view of the continent's predicament.

In the face of historical injustices and the lingering impact of colonization, a clear truth emerges: Africa's transformation demands a holistic approach. The principles presented throughout this book offer a roadmap toward progress, each illuminating a path that, when woven together, creates a mosaic of equitable development and inclusive growth.

The call to build resilient economies, embrace technological innovation, and foster sustainable urbanization is a call to action that resonates across these pages. The intricacies of public-private partnerships and innovation ecosystems weave a narrative of collaboration that bridges gaps and envisions an empowered future. These principles are not isolated fragments; rather, they form a united front against the challenges that have hindered Africa's progress.

Yet, the journey does not end with principles alone. The vision for Africa's economic future is not a distant dream; it is a tangible reality that requires concerted effort, commitment, and shared purpose. The culmination of this voyage is not an endpoint but a beginning—a call to embrace the ideals presented within these pages and transform them into actionable change.

This conclusion is not a farewell, but a call to arms—a call to carry forward the wisdom and narratives contained within "Rich but Poor." It is a reminder that Africa's economic potential is not an illusion, but an opportunity waiting to be seized. This journey may have its challenges, but it is guided by the principles that have been unveiled—a path illuminated by the determination to overcome historical burdens, the creativity to harness cultural richness, and the dedication to establish just governance.

As we close the book on "Rich but Poor," let it not mark an end, but rather a new beginning—an invitation to embody the principles, cultivate collaboration, and drive innovation. Let the vision for Africa's economic future be our compass, guiding us toward a horizon of prosperity, resilience, and shared advancement.

"Rich but Poor" is not just a collection of words; it's a manifesto for change, a declaration of intent to rise above challenges and embrace opportunities. It encapsulates the belief that Africa's wealth extends beyond its resources to encompass the potential of its people. Armed with this book, let us step confidently into the future, equipped with insights, principles, and a collective determination to shape Africa's destiny on our own terms.

Pethias Katampi

www.ingramcontent.com/pod-product-compliance
Lightning Source LLC
LaVergne TN
LVHW090423210926
848480LV00002B/660

* 9 7 9 8 2 3 2 4 2 0 3 9 0 *